D0001466

No More Silly Love Songs

No More Silly Love Songs

A Realist's Guide to Romance

Anouchka Grose

Portobello
BOOKS

Published by Portobello Books Ltd 2010

Portobello Books Ltd
Twelve Addison Avenue
London
W11 4QR

A CIP catalogue record for this book is available from the British Library

9 8 7 6 5 4 3 2

ISBN 978 1 84627 186 1

www.portobellobooks.com

Text design and typesetting in Filosophia by Lindsay Nash

Printed and bound in the UK by CPI Mackays, Chatham ME5 8TD

For Martin

LOVE IS THE MAGICIAN THAT PULLS MAN OUT
OF HIS OWN HAT.

Ben Hecht

Contents

Contents

Introduction

It would be reasonable to say that the last thing the world needs is yet another book about love. It would also be reasonable to speculate that without love there would be no books in the first place – so who's going to quibble about one more?

The human tendency to bond and fight is at the heart of our culture. We seem to have a burning need to speak, write and sing about attachment and separation: what brings people together, and what makes them break apart. The great thing about books, songs, films and poems about love is that they don't even have to be very different. Love is such a pressing issue for humanity that the subtlest variations seem to matter. The charts are always full of records detailing the intricacies of the first six months of romance. You wanna dance with somebody, you can't get them out of your head, you've really got the feeling, and so on. And then there's the aftermath: you're never gonna dance again, you're leaving on a jet plane and every day you love them less and less. Extreme emotions are charmingly packaged into accessible – and often strangely addictive – blocks of sound. They're all a bit similar and a bit dissimilar. Love songs also make endless attempts to define exactly what love is: *Love is Strange*, *Love is Like a Butterfly*, *Love is Noise*, *Love is Hell*, *Love is All There is*, *Love is My Religion*, *Love is a Number*, *Love is a Losing Game*, *Pain is Love*, *Love is a Serious Business*, *Love is Blue*, *Love is Only Love*... If you can convincingly pin down something, anything about the experience of linking or unlinking yourself with another human being then you are providing a useful service. Thank you Burt Bacharach, Dolly Parton, Björn and Benny. Not to mention Shakespeare, Proust and Barbara Cartland. As a subject, love has proved equally inspirational for poets, novelists, playwrights and film directors. Our appetite for stories about love appears to be inexhaustible.

For scientists too, it's a compelling topic. According to modern science, love has been essential to our survival and evolution as a species. Recent developments in neuroscience give us new ways of thinking about the chemical make-up of love. It's even been suggested that we give poetry a break and try to think more seriously about the mechanics of the whole business. Instead of hearts and flowers we apparently need to be thinking along the lines of hormones and neurotransmitters. Humans are basically breeding machines that function according to their programming. An appealing member of the opposite sex (assuming we don't possess the mythical 'gay gene', presumably) will trigger a chemical rush in us, inducing an attraction. If both parties are available they can act on this triggering and have sex. And if they procreate, then more chemicals will be released in order to ensure that they love their baby and each other. But as you can see from the way humans actually live, this machinery functions far from impeccably.

So, are literature and lyrics just part of an illusion that blinds us to the physical realities of attraction? Are all these words written in order to describe something that is already there, or do they magic it into existence? While some writers define love as a basic human need, there are also those who see it as a product of our culture – something that was invented quite late in human development. Some historians and anthropologists would argue that love as we know it dates back to the Middle Ages, or that each period and society invents its own notion of love. What passed for love in the European courts of the eleventh century may have little to do with the practices of contemporary New Guinean tribes, or with the world of the heart so acutely described by Amy Winehouse. There's animal attraction and then there's what we do with it, which are not at all the same thing.

This question of natural or unnatural is brilliantly played out in Baz Luhrmann's *Moulin Rouge!* Apparently the film was conceived as one long, relentless cliché about love. Any narrative element that deviated from the norm was erased in favour of what was totally generic. It's the story of a young romantic who falls in love with a prostitute with very 'realistic' ideas about love. He thinks it's the best thing about life and that you just have to do it for no reason. She thinks it's a great way to squeeze money out of stupid, rich men. She has a confusing moment when she mistakes him for a rich man, but actually likes him, and then finds out that he's a penniless writer. So he sets out to persuade her to love him for nothing. They stand on a roof and Ewan McGregor strikes out with a barrage of lines from famous love songs by Kiss, U2, Joe Cocker, the Beatles, Dolly Parton, David Bowie, and whoever else has written a romantic number that half the world might be expected to recognize. When Satine, the prostitute (played by Nicole Kidman), finally has enough of McGregor's warbling she fires back a line from Paul McCartney's 'Silly Love Songs', to the effect that enough's enough. McGregor's character, Christian, is unfazed and keeps singing. And eventually it seems to work. Satine is brought round by the power of song (and cliché). But the argument has been set up: is love a sublime and mysterious force that we should submit to? Or is it part of a more pragmatic system of exchange? And, perhaps more confusingly, which is more natural and which more artificial? Is Christian following his instincts while Satine suppresses hers for financial gain? Or is it the other way round? Don't animals mate according to the economics of attractiveness – better looks get you better stuff? And isn't pure, unadulterated romantic love a bizarre human artifice?

Satine's objection to love songs seems to be that they make love appear one way, whereas the reality is something quite other. She's certain that romantic love can't last and that, if they get together, Christian will be mean to her and she'll start drinking. In other words she has the idea that love is just a temporary mirage that binds you to another person and that, once bound, you can only be unhappy. (A concept that can be biochemically backed up, if you're so inclined.) According to Satine, the best thing to do is to use the blinding illusion to extract what you can – and then disappear. Although she is eventually unable to resist Christian's charms, the film finishes with her dying in his arms, having just declared her love for him. Things don't get a chance to turn sour between them and the fantasy of enduring love is sustained. The overall message of the film seems to be that love is extremely compelling, but it doesn't necessarily lead to anything good. In fact it promises precisely nothing – that's the point. It's just a very powerful force that you have to give in to when it inexplicably steams your way.

But having opted to give in to love, what happens next (assuming you don't immediately die of consumption)? This book tries to say something about what you might be able to expect from love in a society where pretty much anything is allowed. You can be gay or straight, monogamous or polygamous, married or single – in any combination that you think will work for you. You can dress up as a horse and pull your lover around the living room in a chariot, if you like. And, whatever you're into, you can supposedly use the Internet to find other people to do it with you. There's no longer any stable idea of what love is or how to go about it. Instead there's an infinite number of options, all with their upsides and downsides. The choices can appear overwhelming.

And then there's always the question of whether you genuinely *have* a choice. Maybe it's more a matter of being honest with yourself about who you unavoidably are. Polygamy (or, for others, dressing up as a horse) may seem exotic, but is it something you are constitutionally suited to? What is it that you genuinely *like*? And would doing it actually make you happy, or is it better off left as a fantasy? Should you even expect your sentimental life to bring you happiness or would it be better to accept that love is all about moderating disappointment?

Each chapter will try to deal with a different aspect of love. Why does it so often make you miserable? Or crazy? What is the case for and against monogamy? Is marriage a good idea? Are men and women really different when it comes to love? How do you know when it's time to split up? There will be very little by way of advice, and lots of hair-tearing confusion. But it seems that you need to be prepared to be a bit perplexed if you take the subject seriously. If anyone tells you they have a solution to the problem of love, don't let them anywhere near your wallet. It's a mess and, to paraphrase Leonard Cohen, there definitely ain't no cure. But the worse it is, the more there is to say, and the more it seems worth saying.

The ideas in this book are pooled from a number of sources. There's the mountain of poems, songs, philosophical texts, films and novels that deal with the subject of love – although it can be hard to tell whether these are a hindrance or a help. There's also a bit of science. Then there's the fact that I am a psychoanalyst, so am constantly in discussion with people about their extraordinary, difficult and puzzling love lives. These people are all betting on the idea that speaking about it can somehow help. In some cases it seems to. In others it's harder to see progress – but then again you don't know how much worse things might have been if they hadn't had someone to talk to. (The classic shrinks' get-out clause.) Sometimes people manage to find amazing, ingenious solutions to their seemingly intractable problems. These solutions don't always last, but they can be impressive while they do. In any case, lots of words get exchanged on the subject of love and at least some of them might reassure us that no matter how tormented we might be feeling, we're not completely alone.

Lastly, and most pressingly, at least for me, I have unavoidably drawn ideas from my own messy life. There is nothing that pushes people to write more than romantic troubles. And even a decade of psychoanalysis won't necessarily save you from these. I had no plans to write a book about love until the person I was going out with did something that really upset me. I suspected I was being a bit unreasonable, but then again anyone I mentioned it to said, 'Oh no, poor you!' While it seemed mad to be suffering so much over something so stupid, it was a kind of madness that made sense to other people. I didn't know what to do with myself, so I rang him and shouted at him. This didn't help the situation very much. So instead of carrying on shouting I spent a couple of days scribbling in a notepad like a teenager, trying to understand something about what love was and why it felt so awful. Then I compressed the ramblings into an email, sent it to an editor, and this is the result. I'm saying this for two reasons. One, it will partially explain why the book is a bit pessimistic in places. And two, I feel the need to justify its existence. It's certainly not the case that I am any more of an authority on the subject than anyone else. Being a psychoanalyst doesn't put you in a position of superior knowledge, it just means you believe it's worthwhile to think about unsavoury and difficult things. I am not an expert on anything. Like most people who have tried to say something about love I did it because I didn't know what else to do. It seemed to help somehow. And if a lover ever does anything that seriously distresses you I'd really recommend it. It's much better than cutting up their clothing – or your own wrists for that matter.

When I began this book I had one burning question about love: 'why bother?' Based on the pain I was feeling, it seemed to me a question worth asking. I already have a very excellent daughter, and am not especially keen to have another. I have much better friends than I deserve. There is the question of sex, but then some of the more open-minded of these friends had even offered to help out with that. There seemed no obvious reason to go through the very painful and difficult process of getting seriously involved with another person – apart from the fact that without that kind of intimacy life could start to seem a bit surface-skimming and dull.

But then when you dipped below the surface with anyone it was scary. Perhaps more so after nearly a decade of marriage, and the few garbled attempts at relationships that followed. You could almost see the ending before the beginning. And anyone genuinely interesting had even more hang-ups about it than me. All my single friends were in the same boat. And lots of my couple friends were pretty troubled about the whole business too, only for different reasons.

But 'why bother?' also seemed like a question worth *answering*. There are clearly plenty of reasons to bother – and some of them extend so far beyond us and our own small, particular existences that they are worth constantly bearing in mind. It stopped being a question about what to do on a Saturday night and became a series of questions about what human beings are and what they might be trying to do with each other. And this seemed to be a better way to think about the difficulties and satisfactions of a relationship than silly stuff about who buys the cinema tickets or whether your partner remembers anniversaries. Love really is a serious business and giving up isn't an option that most of us want to live with long term. Whatever happens, there always seems to be a reason (or a temptation) to have another go. In a sense, trying to answer the question of why we bother was my nutty, temporary solution to the problem of romance. While some of my patients try multiple dating, painting, platonic sleeping together, binge eating, having babies, marriage, overwork and casual sex in their attempts to solve their problems around attachment, I tried this.

If an analyst writes a book about love, you have to expect Freud to get the odd mention. But there seems to be a widely held notion that Freud got it all wrong. Even people who pay to turn up to analysis twice a week sometimes think this. It seems to me that this would be a bit like saying that Shakespeare got it all wrong. Of course, Shakespeare didn't try to back up his extraordinary insights into the human psyche with science. He can afford to be mistaken or 'sexist' because he doesn't have the scary armature of nineteenth-century paternalistic pig-headedness to make it seem really offensive. But as well as saying some peculiar things about women Freud also listened to them, particularly concerning the problems in their sentimental lives, and then thought extremely hard about what they said. Freud's ideas about love, sex and attachment go way beyond people's early childhood experiences and right back to the primeval swamps. His theories are beautiful and gloomy and seem to me to explain much more than most contemporary theories of attraction, which barely scratch the surface. So this book won't bring you all the latest psychological findings on this and that, because the latest findings are so often so boring and so completely lacking in either perception or poetry that they're better off left alone. Who cares if someone has just written a paper about why nasty men are more popular with women? While newspapers and women's magazines might be full of this stuff, it rarely seems to explain anything. You hand over your £3.60 and then wish you'd invested it in parmesan or socks. (But then you recant *immediately* if the magazine has also secured an interview with ALL THREE of the Sugababes.) So while Freud may be considered completely uncool, I really hope I've been able to make some sort of case for taking him seriously. Reading contemporary psychology is unlikely to move you in the way a song can. I've never been addicted to an article in the *British Journal of Psychology* like I can get hooked on a pop record. But Freud is up there with the best songwriters in that he really seems to be trying to articulate something about existence in a way that your average researcher or compiler of surveys is unlikely ever to be able to manage. His theories can seem a bit extreme and unwieldy, but in terms of having something to say about the problems of love he's as good as Leonard Cohen.

So here are my distorted and outmoded ideas about love and contemporary life. I hope that some of them chime with yours, that some of them are quite different from yours, and that some of them really annoy you. That way at least we'll be having something like a worthwhile relationship. And you can always leave me – or write a book or a song of your own.

1.

Have I Told You Lately That I Love You?

What do we mean by 'love'?

♥ ♥

*In which we contemplate etymology, ancient philosophy,
anthropology and knights in shining armour*

IF YOU SAY 'I LOVE YOU' THEN YOU HAVE ALREADY
FALLEN IN LOVE WITH LANGUAGE, WHICH IS
ALREADY A FORM OF BREAK-UP AND INFIDELITY.

Jean Baudrillard

You are lying in bed next to your boyfriend, your wife, your boyfriend's wife, whoever. You are suddenly swamped by emotion. You want them to know what you are feeling. You wonder whether they may even be feeling something like it too. You try to think how to say it. 'My insides feel disrupted, but in a semi-pleasant, non-physical way, and it seems to have something to do with you.' Too unromantic – and they may just think you have a hangover. 'No other person on this planet excites me as much as you do.' Better, but you haven't met everyone on the planet so you are laying yourself open to charges of insincerity. 'There is something mysterious and precious about you. I can't name it or describe it, but it gets to me. I want to rip you apart, to devour you, to invade your body by osmosis. I want to tear your hair and bite your cheeks, and then to wash you in daffodil juice.' Maybe some people would like to hear this, but it's risky. You don't want to frighten them off at the exact moment you are trying to tell them how much you like them. You decide to be more traditional. At least this way you will get your point across clearly and it won't turn into a display of your verbal dexterity.

'I love you.'

There is a pause. Maybe the other person smiles. Perhaps they look into your eyes. Possibly they say, 'I love you too.' But then again maybe they don't. Either way you wonder what the hell you've just done. Your lover suddenly becomes strange to you. Even their irises look weird. Maybe you've upset them – or, just as bad, maybe you'll never get rid of them now. Do you really love *them*, or just the idea of love itself? Who are they, and what is love anyway? You should have stuck to option number three. At least that way they would have grasped the idea that whatever it is, it isn't necessarily all good.

The word 'love' stems from the Old English word 'lufu', meaning love, affection or friendliness. This in turn grew out of the Pre-Germanic 'lubo', the Old Frisian 'liaf' and the Gothic 'liufs', meaning 'dear' or 'beloved'. There is also the much older Sanskrit word 'lubhyati', meaning 'desires'. (And that's before you get onto all the other etymological journeys the concept has taken – from Latin 'amor', to modern English 'amorous', via French 'amour'. Or from Greek 'Eros' to contemporary 'erotica'. Or 'philia' – a dispassionate, virtuous form of love – which now gives us necrophilia, coprophilia and a whole load of other delightful tendencies.) When you say 'I love you' you are joining in a centuries-long game of Chinese whispers, passing on a series of phonemes to the next person, hoping you didn't screw up too badly. If in the future people find themselves saying 'I loaf you' it will only be partly your fault.

You may have got the sounds right, but what exactly were you trying to get at? It's not just the word 'love' that's changed, it's also the definition. While in the eighth century 'lufu' appears to have been a gentle emotion, by the sixteenth century the word 'lovesick' emerges, attesting to a more uncomfortable feeling. A century after that, you get 'lovelorn', the addition of the Latin 'loren' bringing out the idea that love can make you a loser. So what happened in the intervening millennium to bring about this shift from pleasant to painful? What other words did the Goths have to speak about the misery of attachment? What might we mean by 'love' now? How much does it differ between one culture and another, between one person and another, between ourselves yesterday and today? Is there anything stable about the concept? And, if not, why do so many people choose to say 'I love you' when there is a multitude of other flawed and alienating words to choose from?

Fools for Love

Although there may be little general agreement as to what love *is*, there is a long-held suspicion that it may have some effect on one's good judgement. In short, it can make you either very clever or very stupid. Greek philosophy and Buddhism – which developed roughly simultaneously in the fifth and sixth centuries BC – seem to have opposing takes on this. In Plato's *Symposium*, each of the seven speakers may have different ideas about Eros, but they are all largely of the opinion that love is somehow linked to creation, beauty and the philosophical quest for truth. On the other hand, Buddhism teaches us that romantic attachment can be an obstacle on the path to enlightenment. Is it that Buddhists and Platonists have radically conflicting notions of love? Or are they ultimately saying pretty much the same thing?

Plato's *Symposium* takes place one drunken night in Athens, when the tragic poet Agathon's dinner guests are invited to speak about love. The first of the monologues belongs to Phaedrus, who tells us that love makes people capable of great heroism. Pausanias then goes on to explain the legal situation regarding pederasty. (He basically says it's great, as long as the boy is going along with it for intellectual or virtuous reasons and not in the pursuit of money or power.) Eryximachus discusses medicine and puts forward a theory about the right kind of love regulating body temperature and humidity. Then Aristophanes gives his famous speech about blob-shaped, cartwheeling creatures being cut in half by Zeus, from which comes the popular idea that the search for love is the search for one's missing other half. Next Agathon talks about the marvellousness of the God Eros, after which Socrates hits back with a series of questions undermining the notion of love as straightforwardly good and noble. Finally Alcibiades wanders in and rants drunkenly about Socrates' sexy inner statues. (Much like your average night round at the neighbours, then.) The point here is that, while all the speakers apparently have a different conception of romantic or erotic love, none of them are trying to persuade you not to do it. Quite the opposite. Even Socrates, who presents the lover as someone needy and lacking, capable of deceit and manipulation, is very much behind the idea that an experience of erotic love can set you to work, make you think, study and create.

Socrates begins by getting Agathon to agree to a series of propositions whose general drift is that love is the desire for something one doesn't have. A tall person wouldn't desire to be tall and a healthy person wouldn't desire health. (They might wish to continue to be tall or healthy in the future, but the future hasn't arrived yet, so these hoped-for qualities aren't actually in their possession.) Therefore, according to the tricky logic of Socrates' argument, if one loves/desires things because they are beautiful and good it follows that love itself is neither beautiful nor good. But precisely because love aims at what it doesn't have, it can propel people in interesting and fruitful directions. Socrates claims to have learnt everything he knows from a wise woman called Diotima, and goes on to tell us what she taught him. She has the idea that love is linked with a quest for immortality, explaining it like this:

Haven't you noticed what a terrible state animals of all kinds (footed beasts as well as winged birds) get into when they feel the desire to reproduce? They are all sick with the excitement of love, that makes them first want to have

sex with each other and then to rear what they have
brought into being.

… Mortal nature does all it can to live for ever and to be
immortal. It can only do this by reproduction: it always
leaves behind another new generation to replace the old.

But in case it appears as though she's simply saying that love
makes you want to jump on people so you can have lots of babies,
Diotima makes a very important distinction. There are some
people who are pregnant in body – meaning that love simply
makes them want to breed. And then there are people who are
pregnant in mind. If a person of this type is lucky he'll meet
another mind worthy of triggering mind-babies – i.e. poems,
artworks, mathematical theories, etc. The great thing about
mind-babies is that not only do they not wake you up at four in
the morning, they are also 'more beautiful and more immortal'
than your average brat. 'Everyone would prefer to have children
like that,' she tells Socrates. So her idea is that the 'terrible state'
you get into when you come across someone you desire can cause
you to produce something worthwhile. Using the perceived good
qualities of the other person, you can come up with stuff you
could never have managed alone. Something in the relation will
make it possible for you to make, think or do extraordinary
things. If you perform the rites of love correctly you might even
'reach the final vision of the mysteries'.

So far so encouraging, but here's where it all goes a bit
Buddhist. There is a very specific order in which one's romantic/

erotic life must proceed, otherwise it will all amount to nothing. In the first place it helps to be a very good-looking young boy. In this state an older – and very brilliant – man must fall in love with you. You love him back and have loads of great conversations, during which he opens you up to all manner of big ideas.

Soon you realize that if you are going to admire a man for the beauty of his body, it's only rational that you should love all similarly beautiful bodies equally. You stop being stuck on one body and begin to value beauty in a more objective way. You soon understand that beauty of mind is more important than beauty of body. In fact you become interested in all forms of beauty, such as the beauty of law, or of nature. At last you realize that it's pointless to fixate on any single instance of beauty. It's all the same to you. Beauty becomes an uncontaminated notion, and you can finally appreciate it 'absolute, pure, unmixed, not cluttered up with human flesh and colours and a great mass of mortal rubbish'.

But to reach these heights, you have to fall in love with the clever guy in the first place. It takes a proper experience of erotic love to lead you to the point where a nice bottom and a pair of well-angled cheekbones no longer mean anything to you. A love affair needs to happen in order to supplement your shortcomings, to train your mind in new directions, and ultimately to teach you that love affairs aren't the solution. (Naturally, you may find yourself obliged to make pretty young men fall in love with you in order to keep the system rolling, but you will now be in a position to do this in an appropriately disinterested way.)

♥

So how is this different to the teachings of Buddhism, which also warn against the perils of exclusive erotic attachments? Why do Buddhists have a reputation for being down on romance? This rather brutal quote from the Buddha might begin to explain it:

I have killed all of you before.

I was chopped up by all of you in previous lives.

We have all killed each other as enemies.

So why should we be attached to each other?

(Try saying that to the next lecherous drunk who accosts you in a bar.)

Romantic attachment is an exaggerated form of not wanting to be separated from someone. You imagine that losing your loved one would be the end of your life, or at least the end of your happiness. In this sense, it's no less foolish than being attached to a big bag of money. According to Buddhist ideology, attachment is one of the key things that keeps us captive in samsara. We have to lose our attachments to everything – to people, possessions, even to life itself – if we are ever to achieve enlightenment and not just get stuck in a loop of endless, tedious rebirths. (Oh no! Don't say I've come back as a limpet *again*!) And it's not simply because attachments are fundamentally pointless, but also because they can make us behave badly. We get so stuck on someone that it seems we can only be happy if they are there, being nice to us. We try to make it obvious to them that our well-being is in their hands. We present it as a compliment:

'You are so lovely and brilliant and nice that I can't live without you!' But this compliment is something of a Trojan horse. It makes the other person responsible for us. If they remove their presence we are sad. And it's their fault. They know how we feel about them. How could they do this to us? Why did they have to stay at work late/go and see a friend/climb a mountain? We'll get back at them later. We'll teach them what suffering is, let them see how it feels to be abandoned. We might do this in a number of ways: give them a glum look, be a bit monosyllabic, pick a fight, snog their best friend. The important thing is that we make them feel as miserable as we do. How dare they be happy when we are in so much pain?

Of course Buddhists can fall in love. They just have to work out a way to do it without making their own and the other person's life hell. The generic Buddhist advice is to make a clear distinction between selfish attachment and a more altruistic kind of love. If you can focus on the other person's happiness without fretting too much about your own, then you may have some hope of continuing to be good for each other. The problem with attachment is that it is fundamentally self-seeking. In extreme cases, the other person is simply there to fulfil your needs, make you feel good about yourself, tell you they love you and generally fill up the gaping void that is your inner being. They are never going to achieve this impossible feat, so meanwhile you can berate them. You have someone to blame for your unhappiness, which stops you taking responsibility for it yourself. Well done!

Instead, you could try thinking about who your partner is, and what they might need or like. And, as long as you haven't chosen to build a life with an autocratic monster, then things might turn out okay. Best of all you can get together with another compassionate Buddhist and live undemandingly ever after. Perhaps you can even practise Tantric Buddhism and reach sexual nirvana. In fact it sounds so obvious it's amazing that all relationships aren't happy. Be nice to each other – it's that simple. Or is it? If marriage is so great, then why did the Buddha find it necessary to walk out on his own in order to pursue his spiritual practices?

The story of Siddhartha and Yasodhara's marriage is somewhere just below Dido and Aeneas in the pain stakes. Siddhartha was born the son of Queen Maya and King Suddhodana, towards the end of the sixth century BC. It was pretty obvious that he was special from the start – it was a painless birth (in the garden) and he could walk and talk immediately. Straight away weird things started happening: the statues in the temple prostrated themselves and a great ascetic came to visit. It was clear that this was no ordinary child. A week later Queen Maya died and her sister stepped in to bring up the baby. As any psychoanalyst would tell you, this boy's life was never going to be easy.

When Siddhartha was twelve, a council of Brahmans predicted that if he witnessed old age, sickness and death – and if he met a hermit – then he would become a great ascetic himself. King Suddhodana didn't like the sound of this at all and began laying on the treats, doing everything possible to make his son's home life pleasant. He believed that if he hid everything bad from his beloved son, then he might save him from having to run off and become a penniless recluse.

One of the biggest treats was Yasodhara herself, the most beautiful princess in the land. As teenagers, Siddhartha and Yasodhara were married. They continued to live in incredible luxury at the palace, behind three walls, surrounded by people who were forbidden to mention death or grief. (It was a sort of early precursor of *The Truman Show*.) Unsurprisingly, Siddhartha became curious about the local town and decided to pay it a visit. Despite great stage management on the part of his father, he nonetheless stumbled across the sick and the elderly, the homeless and the dead. The game was up. The world was far more complex and fascinating than he'd ever been allowed to know. Immediately, he wanted to leave the palace and become a beggar.

Devastated by the prospect of losing his son, the king's answer to this was to crank up the festivities and employ more guards. At which point Yasodhara gave birth to a son. Siddhartha's immediate response was 'A rahu is born – a fetter has arisen', so he named his son Rahula, meaning 'fetter'. (And some children complain about being called Archie or Gwendolen!) That night, after one last tender look at his wife and fetter, Siddhartha left the palace, shaved his head and became a monk. From then on Yasodhara lived in misery, getting occasional news reports on her errant husband and copying everything he did – eating one meal a day from a shabby bowl and dressing in yellow robes. When he came to visit years later, she cried all over his feet. Still, she soon came round to the idea that hers wasn't such a bad lot. She had apparently absorbed his ascetic ideals so thoroughly that it all made perfect sense to her.

Of course, hiding all the bad stuff from someone is bound to give them a very special take on life, love and happiness. No wonder the poor man needed to go off and have a serious think. But why did he have to abandon Yasodhara and the hideously named Rahula? Couldn't they have stuck together and explored the nature of being, as a family? Why should knitting one's existence to someone else's necessarily stand in the way of true enlightenment? Is there something in the very fact of being with other people that inevitably generates pettiness? Will there always be a sock-tidier, a chronic snorer or a nag?

Both the Buddha and Socrates seem to agree that it doesn't make sense to get too stuck on someone. But they certainly don't think that the solution is therefore to spread it around. It's quite clear that, according to either philosophy, it would be no less stupid to try to squeeze satisfaction from ten people than from one. The problem is trying to use your fellow humans to get any satisfaction at all. Good things can happen between people, but only people who aren't trying to claw good things out of each other. But the fact that Siddhartha chose to leave his wife in order to achieve Buddhahood is a sign that this isn't so easy. It's not like you can simply say, 'I'm going to stop being an idiot now and start being reasonable.' If you could, people wouldn't have to tell stories about painless births, gesticulating statues and lights shooting out of bodies (as is said to have happened when Siddhartha finally became a Buddha). There is something really very extreme about the whole notion of enlightenment. Pretty much no one in real life ever actually makes it. Especially not those of us who aren't monks. We are just stuck in samsara, doing other people's washing up, listening to their complaints and exacting various levels of revenge on them. It's extremely rare, if not totally unheard of, for people to be consistently decent and happy. You can try very hard to behave yourself in a relationship, but something irritating or impossible will generally seep out. If the Buddha couldn't do it with Yasodhara (who, by all accounts, was a very special woman) then who are we to imagine we might fare any better?

Divine Intervention

Before Greek philosophers and Buddhists started concerning themselves with the problem of love, the Sumerians and Phoenicians worshipped love goddesses – Innana and Astarte respectively. Both these goddesses were concerned not only with love and sex, but also with war, and supposedly went round making all sorts of mess. The Greek goddess Aphrodite and, later, the Roman Venus carried on this tradition. In the myth, Aphrodite was so beautiful that it was feared she would cause trouble among the other gods. So Zeus married her off to the most boring and unsexy god – the club-footed blacksmith, Hephaestus. She got on with being unfaithful to him, while also making trouble for mortals. As the story goes, the Trojan War was started largely thanks to her meddling. She promised Helen of Troy to Paris, infuriating Hera and Athena (who already had it in for Paris for thinking Aphrodite was prettier than them). She also made Pygmalion fall in love with a statue, and caused Myrrha to feel so crazed with lust for her own father that she disguised herself as a prostitute in order to have sex with him. Plus she persuaded Eros to go after Psyche with his golden arrows, with the aim of making her fall in love with the ugliest man in the world. So you could say that Aphrodite/Venus was generally quite bad news. And those nice, chubby cupids you see floating around in Renaissance paintings and on greetings cards are no better; Cupid is simply Venus' evil sidekick.

But if the Greeks and Romans glorified Eros, or erotic love, and all the chaos it can bring, the Christians were supposedly far more interested in agape, a self-sacrificing form of love. Agape can refer to the kind of benevolent love God might feel for his creatures. And to the kind of love the creatures might feel back. The hope is that they might also learn to love each other in this way and then there would be no more need for Trojan wars, etc., because humanity would have become so nice. (The Crusades, the slaughter of the Incas, the Spanish Inquisition, witch-hunts and the rest were minor aberrations, naturally.) Christians, like Buddhists, were encouraged to calm down and try to be decent to each other. And the more decent they were to each other, and the more self-sacrificingly they loved their God, the more likely they would be to go to heaven. Chasing after earthly enjoyments was presented as a bad idea. If you could just hold off being desperate and grasping in life, you'd be much better rewarded in death. So Christian marriages weren't sold on the grounds of being exciting. Quite the opposite. They were a means of producing children, serving God and avoiding sin. Half the point in Christian marriage was to save you from being tempted to do anything too interesting.

Greek philosophers, Buddhists, Taoists, Jews, Christians and Muslims all seem to have come up with loosely analogous strategies for dealing with love. There's a broad consensus that you can love someone truly and deeply, but should try to avoid the madly. On the face of it, this might sound like good advice. But the problem with most good advice is that if it were really any good, it would soon become redundant. Everyone would just say, 'You're right', and that would be the end of it. The fact that religious preachers, relationship counsellors and magazine writers still regularly find it necessary to tell us to be a bit more cool-headed is surely a sign that the message isn't arriving. Is it because no one's quite managed to find quite the right way to phrase it? Or because there's a great deal of resistance to hearing it? And if people seem to *want* to suffer in love, are there some doctrines or ideologies that actually recommend it?

In twelfth-century Europe a strange poetic tradition began to emerge. The stories it dealt with apparently had very little to do with the sorts of things real people actually got up to, but audiences liked them anyway. They were written in vernacular French, as opposed to the older and more 'literary' Latin. This new language – developed out of Latin – was known as 'romanz'. The poems dealt with the themes of love and longing played out between married ladies and their husbands' noble knights. They were written and performed by troubadours – travelling poets who stayed at court under the patronage of the lord. Troubadours were particularly popular with female members of court, who were less involved in killing people and animals, and therefore needed something to do. While German epic poetry – with which most European princesses would have been acquainted – was largely about men being brave while the women lurked in the background, these new poems depicted powerful, desirable female characters. They were therefore extremely popular.

The crux of the tradition of the courtly love poem (and perhaps of courtly love itself, although it's uncertain that any real, live people actually practised it) is that a knight is madly in love with a very virtuous married lady and has to perform tasks in order to please her. Meanwhile she won't deign to so much as kiss him. The knight believes that one of the things that will really impress the lady is his unflinching devotion to his liege lord (her husband). So he goes out of his way to be the most faithful, brave and honourable knight ever. In the course of winning the approval of this inaccessible female beauty he becomes a decent and morally uplifted young man.

This type of story is said to have fulfilled a few very important functions. It presented men with a model of good behaviour. This is thought to have been particularly important at the time because of the inheritance customs. Eldest sons tended to get pretty much everything, meaning that younger brothers often couldn't afford to marry. They generally had to choose between becoming priests or becoming knights. As a result, you had all these angry younger siblings charging around the countryside, drunk and sexually frustrated, causing a terrible social nuisance, jumping on women and getting into brawls. (And that's just the priests.) If only you could persuade them that they were actually getting quite a good deal, that it was a better bet to be an ideal lover than a boring old husband, then you might be able to keep them in check. Women supposedly liked the stories because it all sounded a lot more fun than the sorts of compulsory baby-making activities they got up to with their husbands, who had generally been chosen by their parents.

So, courtly love came to be defined by a number of key characteristics: it had to happen between aristocrats, otherwise it was just plain extra-marital flirting. It had to follow certain codes of etiquette concerning the exchanging of letters, love tokens, etc. The husband had to be kept in the dark – the illicit-ness was half the point. And there had to *be* a husband in the first place, otherwise the lovers might just end up marrying (which wouldn't be courtly at all). In other words, you needed a large number of obstacles. In a sense, the obstacles became the point. This different sort of love arrangement, ostensibly unconsummated – although even in a lot of the poems it's fairly clear that the lovers are getting up to *something* – certainly undomesticated, got its very potency from its fundamental impossibility. The man had to act like the woman was too mighty and virtuous ever to succumb to his advances. And the woman could get off on the idea of some dashing guy being nuts about her, without the risk of her ever having to give birth or darn his socks. And in that state of nothing much happening, everything could happen. The two of them could wilt and pine and dream and write little notes and go happily insane in the manner that we now call 'romantic'.

Of course twelfth-century troubadours weren't the first people to subscribe to the idea that longing and suffering were the good bit, while marriage was a drag. The tradition had a much older precursor in the form of the ghazal, a type of Arabic love poem. Instead of knights and ladies it tended to focus on the love a man might feel for a young slave or soldier. But the flavour was very much the same; the love had to be illicit, the sense of longing and separation very much lingered over and enjoyed. The imagery of the poems was often quite violent, with plenty of exposed and quivering hearts, glistening blades and piercing arrows. The lover wasn't any normal mortal with whom you simply wanted to have sex, but an emissary of the divine. Most of the ghazal poets were either practising Sufis or influenced by Sufism, meaning they believed it was possible to have some kind of close relation to God while still alive. The kind of aching, extreme love portrayed in the ghazal is a mystical experience, a point of access to the sublime.

So in these poetic traditions it appears that you have to suffer if you really want to get something out of love. But you must suffer in quite a particular way. Nobody is recommending that you tolerate thirty years of excruciating boredom under the same roof as your spouse. Instead you must have very little access to your lover at all. And this highly mediated relation to your love object will bring you extraordinary, intense spiritual euphoria.

While many religions preach the idea that you should aim to be even-tempered in love, it often turns out that there is a variant version of the doctrine that recommends exactly the opposite. In the same way that Sufism has its particular take on Islam, so too can you find erotic-love-promoting tendencies in Buddhism, Taoism and certain forms of Christian mysticism.

We'll discuss later why separation and obstacles might be necessary components of romance, but for now the aim is just to bring out the two different approaches to love. On one side you have the tendency that tells you to calm down, it's only an illusion, it'll pass. And on the other you have the people who think it's best to really milk the intolerable sensations. Which camp you fall into may be decided by inclination, education or both. Your family, community or religion may push you towards one or the other. Indeed, your cultural background is likely to play a considerable role in dictating what you think love is. (Although, ultimately, it can't solve the problem of what you're supposed to do about it.)

Love in a Multitude of Different Climates

In the early 1990s romantic love suddenly became *the* hot new anthropological topic. Of course anthropologists had taken it into consideration before, but there was a widespread consensus that it was a uniquely Western practice, not relevant to other societies. 'Romance' as we know it was invented in eleventh-century Europe, and other cultures did other things. It was believed that in places where arranged marriage was the norm no one would have the slightest idea what might make somebody pull the petals off a daisy or wait around on a street corner hoping for a glimpse of their crush (which is odd given that courtly love flourished in precisely this context).

While you might detect a hint of unconscious racism in all of this – 'What, those people with funny hairstyles experience love too?' – it was all very rationally explained. Romance, in the modern sense, was thought to require a certain level of comfort and leisure time to flourish; you had to be rich and bored to do it properly. Capitalist societies, characterized by the rise of the individual and the collapse of the extended family, were thought to create the perfect breeding ground for this particular brand of love; you didn't have your parents telling you who to marry, and you needed something interesting to fill up your spare time. Any lurking racism was concealed under the politically correct notion that 'we're all so screwed up and decadent in our technologized, individualistic society that we indulge in these silly pastimes to give our empty lives meaning'. The rest of the world, apparently, knows better.

In 1992 William Jankowiak and Edward Fischer published a very influential paper called 'Romantic Love, a Cross-Cultural Perspective'. They felt that the current ethnographic stance on romance was impossibly Eurocentric, not to mention unsustainable in the face of the evidence. In their opinion, anthropologists' fixed notions of what constituted the proper objects of study were getting in the way of their capacity to observe the facts. They were so stuck on finding out about marriage rituals and kinship structures that they'd forgotten to ask about love. Using Murdock and White's standard cross-cultural sample (a study of 186 distinct cultures, from Ancient Babylonians to contemporary Russian Chukchi), Jankowiak and Fischer set out to prove that romantic love existed beyond the confines of Europe in the second millennium. (And, given that it supposedly 'began' with the troubadours appropriating an Arabic poetic tradition, they could hardly fail to be right.) On sifting through the evidence they concluded that around 89 per cent of the cultures on the list showed evidence of romantic love, and that the remaining 11 per cent were inconclusive. They looked at personal interviews, official records, poetry and folklore, and became quite convinced that romantic yearning was all but universal.

How did Jankowiak and Fischer define romance? As an acute idealization of another person that included an erotic dimension, accompanied by the strong wish that some sort of relationship might take place over time. The idea that this sort of experience could be confined to the upper classes, or to industrialized societies, was ludicrous. In trying to explain how anthropologists could have made such a stupid slip, they pointed out that it can be difficult to get at what people *actually* do when the ideals of a society might be so far removed from real life. Just because your culture dictates that you must have a few husbands, it doesn't necessarily follow that this will be what you want. In high Himalayan societies, for instance, the women find themselves facing precisely this predicament. While they are expected to carry on marital relations with a number of men, they often find that they'd rather be allowed to get on with a single, passionate relationship. Their romantic situation is still char-acterized by overvaluation and obstacles – the key obstacle in this case not being chastity, but the duty to service more than one man.

In the introduction to his book, *Intimacies, Love and Sex Across Cultures*, Jankowiak states that every society has to find something to say about the three-part problem of love, sex and companionship. It's almost unheard of for any collection of humans to get together and simply say, 'It's all great – do what you like.' Even hippie sex communes usually have rules. The three sets of needs have to be organized in order to give people some sort of compass points around which to orient their love lives. It's not that they will actually do what society dictates, just that they will have some idea of what's expected of them and position themselves accordingly. Perhaps they will do exactly the opposite. Or maybe they will obey the rules but wish things could be another way.

The puzzle that any culture faces involves choosing what kinds of behaviour to encourage, and what to try to prevent. If the idea is to breed sustainably and to create social bonds that encourage survival (and possibly even make life pleasant) then the issues of love, sex, friendship and family are going to have to be carefully thought through. Inevitably some things will be held up as virtues while others will be denigrated. Some groups elevate the notion of companionship at the expense of sex. Others foreground sex, but in a highly ritualized setting. Some (like the medieval European courts) focus on romance above everything. And then again in Friedrichshof, a 1970s Viennese commune, inhabitants were expected to have sex roughly every four hours, but never with the same partner in a week. No culture has so far managed to find such a great solution that everybody simply fits in with it. In any society there are people who deviate from the norm, and many more who would like to.

Having said that, some solutions may give the appearance of working better than others. In rural China, the mother/son relationship is very highly valued. Boys and their mothers show a degree of intimacy that modern Westerners might find odd. The problem with this particular relationship being so privileged is that it tends to cause difficulties when the son gets married. The mother feels threatened by the arrival of another woman, and the young wife has to suffer the scowls and sulks of her new in-law. As a result, there are very high suicide rates for women in both their twenties and their forties; as they battle for the love of the man, they frequently reach the conclusion that one of them has to go.

Samoan society is more focused on brother/sister bonds — your sibling is always expected to be more important to you than your spouse. Having said that, it's vital that the brother/sister relationship remains asexual. Domestic violence is rife in Samoa, ostensibly because it's very difficult to integrate sex into a relationship that is a mirror image of your non-sexual ideal. You are expected to love your wife like a sister, but also to fuck her. Violence is apparently used as a way of eroticizing a marriage — or at least of somehow making the sexual side of it bearable. In rural China too, wife-beating is extremely common, presumably because it's very difficult for men to suddenly rewrite the rules concerning intimacy and sexuality.

Aka pygmies describe feelings of deep attachment to their wives, at the same time as insisting that it's necessary for them to go out and find other women with whom to have children. Aka wives often attack their husbands in jealous rages, but the men take it philosophically. They can understand why their wives don't want them to sleep around, but that's no reason for them not to go ahead with it anyway.

In New Guinea, men regularly feel so anguished after having sex that they slice their penises with bamboo sticks.

It would be easy to say that all these cultures hadn't found very ingenious ways of organizing love and sex – there's too much pain involved. Or you could say that violence and suffering are simply an integral part of their emotional landscapes, and who are we to advise them otherwise? Have we really managed to come up with anything better?

Any culture can only ever be a bundle of ideas that individuals choose to take seriously or to ignore. Rather than saying, 'The Trobriand islanders do this, while the Manhattanites do that,' you could say that everyone has to work out their own solution in relation to the world around them. Some Himalayan women presumably find ways to fob off their many husbands so they can focus all their affection on the man they really like. Some middle-class British men are far too bound up with their mothers or sisters and it gets in the way of their relationships. Some Aka pygmies probably can't be bothered to go out on the prowl – and maybe even fantasize about seeing their own wives in bed with other men.

While people often want to depict love and romance as something frivolous, even extraneous, it seems that few ideas could be more wrong. Our success or failure as a species is largely dependent on the kinds of relationships we can form. You could see the whole of human history as a series of social experiments, with the management of sexuality at the heart of each trial. So far, no group has managed to resolve the problem perfectly, leaving it down to each one of us to try to come up with a solution of our own. These personal solutions are also liable to fall short – we marry someone we really like but are bored, we change our partners constantly but are lonely, we choose to be celibate but are plagued by inexplicable aches and pains. The question of how best to manage romantic relationships continues to prove unanswerable – but that doesn't stop us trying.

As Seen on TV

Because none of us has found a solution that *really* satisfies, it's likely that we will be very curious about other people's attempts to do the same thing. Have they spotted something we've missed? The fact that governments and private companies see fit to finance anthropological research testifies to the fact that this area of study is deemed worthy of investment. It may benefit us somehow. Either it will bolster a feeling of superiority, or it will present us with new and stealable ideas.

At the same time as treating other cultures as objects of fascination, the West has bombarded the rest of the world with its own notions of the good, the bad and the enjoyable – initially through the medium of conquerors and missionaries, and lately via cinema and TV. The whole world is being force-fed the romantic ideals of a bit of twelfth-century poetry, filtered through Jane Austen before being shot in glorious Technicolor and then digitized for more virulent dissemination. These days it's no longer a surprise to find that the remotest settlements, from Africa to Mongolia, are served by satellite television. But what effect does this have on other peoples? Are we gradually conning the entire world into submitting to our flawed and failing sentimental ideals?

Arranged marriage is one of the key casualties of the cinematic invasion. Assaulted by constant narratives centring on love matches, society after society is finding that its young people won't play along when the time comes to get hitched. This sort of refusal can be extremely perplexing to older generations. In some cultures romantic love is seen as a sorry state requiring immediate treatment; so why on earth would you want to stake your entire future on it? In the mountains of Iran there is a tribe who apparently find it extremely comical when people marry for love. (You may suspect that they are using ridicule as a method of social control. Or you might equally say that they have a point.) Romantic love threatens the entire societal infrastructure. How are you supposed to organize the distribution of cows if young people just pair up according to their whim?

This new tendency towards love matches is triggering a number of strange phenomena. Some societies find themselves experiencing an avalanche of scandalous elopements. Others – notably the Australian Aboriginals – are seeing large numbers of girls 'accidentally' getting pregnant in order to be obliged to marry the man they love. Then again, many cultures have been observed negotiating gentler rules, still arranging marriages but giving participants the right of veto.

Bollywood cinema has a long tradition of playing love matches off against arranged marriages. They've been doing it since the 1930s. The love triangle is a staple of Bollywood movies, with the 'true love' regularly pitted against the partner selected by the family. Although you could say that this is partly thanks to the influence of Hollywood, you might also have to admit that ancient Sanskrit dramatists came up with some pretty good love triangles of their own, a couple of centuries BC. Indeed Bollywood cinema has influenced Western cinema in return, notably *Moulin Rouge!*, which not only includes colour-saturated musical numbers, but also borrows its storyline from a Sanskrit play called *The Little Clay Cart*. So Americans can't take *all* the credit for making other people's love lives difficult.

In the industrialized West, where divorce is rife and romantic marriages are held out to be the norm, one regularly hears about friendships between the in-laws proving more durable than the relationship itself. Society doesn't immediately collapse when people follow their own idiosyncratic wishes. New forms of social arrangement are just produced out of the situation. But there's still the question of why the love match holds so much appeal. We are often told that arranged marriages function very well, that the people involved generally grow to love each other, and that they are far less likely than the rest of us to get divorced. As schemes for a happy life go, it has a lot to be said for it. So why aren't *we* copying *them*? (Perhaps you could say that computer dating, with its information-sifting, matchmaking technology, is a peculiar Western perversion of arranged marriage. The software will select your perfect partner. And maybe computers sometimes get it right – although I was recently impressed and appalled when Facebook singled my ex-husband out as someone I might like to befriend…)

If the image of the princess and the knight in shining armour getting married and living happily ever after has its roots in the tradition of courtly love, it seems that we ought to have grown out of that particular bedtime story by now. (Although it may be quite efficient at sending us to sleep.) In fact, we probably have. Although celebrity magazines may still make reference to 'fairy-tale weddings', they also revel in the acrimonious aftermath. We all understand perfectly well that happy endings are often mere precursors to miserable futures. Love relations are known to be troubled and short-lived. So what makes them look so good on TV? People seem very ready to believe that if you are allowed to choose for yourself, you'll choose better. You'll pick someone you actually like – not someone you have to force yourself to like. It stands to reason that you'll be happier that way. Won't you? It's possible that one of the biggest advantages of arranged marriage – aside from the obvious benefits of social cohesion and property distribution – is that you can blame your parents if your spouse turns out to be a pig. If *you'd* picked them, you'd only have yourself to blame. When arranged marriage doesn't work, you can put it down to something concrete and pragmatic – 'I was forced to marry the bastard because of his gourd plantation.' You are spared the grim idea that love *itself* is the problem. Neither free choice nor arranged marriage offer any guarantee of anything. All we can hope to do is to carry on struggling, cross-pollinating, imitating and stealing in the vain hope that one day somebody will hit upon a strategy that works. Meanwhile, we just have to bear the fact that love is a variable notion. While there's something about it that seems to be universal (and we'll see what the biologists have to say about this later), it can only ever be looked at on a case-by-case basis. If someone tells you they love you, there's no reason to believe that either you or they have any idea what they are on about.

You are in bed with your husband's mistress, your childhood sweetheart, your cousin. They are giving you a funny look. There's a long silence, during which the stare intensifies. It's starting to worry you.

'I love you.'

Oh no! *They* said it. That's even worse.

'You what?' you ask, perplexed.

'I. Love. You. Which bit do you not get?'

'Well, there's the first bit, the last bit and especially the bit in the middle,' you explain.

Their lip twists into a vicious sneer. 'You're so screwed up,' they say. 'I don't know what I'm doing hanging around with you.'

'Yes, I wondered about that too,' you say, and fall into a restless sleep.

2.

Cry Me a River

Why we love to be unhappy in love

♥ ♥

*In which a woman chooses to be unhappy and Schopenhauer
and Sigmund Freud attempt to explain why*

HE MUST HAVE A TRULY ROMANTIC NATURE, FOR
HE WEEPS WHEN THERE IS NOTHING AT ALL TO
WEEP ABOUT.

Oscar Wilde

A woman went into psychoanalysis wondering why she always chose men who made her unhappy. (Sounds like the cue for a joke, only it isn't.) Ava had been married twice – once to a man who'd all but ignored her, and then to a man who watched her obsessively, convinced she was having numerous affairs. Both marriages ended after about four years, with lots of pain and recrimination. Two years after her second marriage ended she met Lucien, who seemed unlike either of her husbands. He was attentive without being overwhelming. And he had very nice hair. He was a screenwriter and she genuinely liked his work. There seemed to be something very calm and kind about him. Despite being rather dubious about love, the woman couldn't see how it could all go wrong this time. She was quite sure it *would*, she just couldn't predict by what means.

She'd met Lucien at a dinner party. He'd arrived with a female friend, Gertrude, and the three of them had had an enjoyable evening together. After that Ava saw Lucien a couple of times, always accompanied by Gertrude – who turned out to be his ex-girlfriend. Ava didn't *mind* Gertrude, but she was rather keen on Lucien and wondered how it might be possible to get to see him alone. (It's amazing that she failed to spot the problem earlier. But she prided herself on her open-mindedness, and knew all about the difficulties that sprang from jealousy. At least this was how she explained it to herself later.)

Finally, Lucien and Ava went on a date. Lucien stayed the night, and they started trying to live happily ever after – in a kind of level-headed way. Both of them had been disappointed before and knew it was a bad idea to have high hopes. But the fact that Lucien was reserved and realistic only made Ava like him more. In fact she liked him a good deal more than she'd initially expected, and found herself embellishing reality, telling herself that this relationship was somehow special. They'd learnt from their past mistakes and wouldn't repeat them. Maybe it really *was* possible for a romance to go well. She didn't even mind occasionally dropping by for a cup of tea with Gertrude at one in the morning, when she'd much rather have been in bed.

After six months of down-to-earth quasi-happiness Lucien and Ava went on a trip to Rome. One of Lucien's films was appearing in a festival. He and Gertrude had worked on it together, so the three of them travelled as a group, staying in the same hotel. During the course of the week Lucien got the bedroom doors mixed up, trying to unlock Gertrude's room instead of his own. Gertrude paired off with a shambling alcoholic and freaked Lucien out, disappearing for whole days and turning up late for screenings. Lucien stood Ava up, failing to meet her at an arranged spot, leaving her confused and miserable. After the main screening of the film (which presented a highly idealized portrait of his previous relationship) Lucien got very drunk and told Ava that he loved Gertrude, that he needed her and that he'd always be there for her. Ava was devastated. She'd known all along that he and Gertrude had keys to each other's flats, that they spoke or saw each other most days and that they shared a room when they went away on trips together. But she hadn't had to witness their relationship so close-up. It was nauseating. Why did they insist on acting like a couple in front of her? Why did Lucien pay for Gertrude's dinners and hotel room, but not hers? Why did Gertrude glue herself to his side all night at the screening party, leaving Ava to talk to the boring alcoholic? Why did Lucien *let* her? When they got back to London Ava tried to dump Lucien. She said that Gertrude was a flaky, self-obsessed bitch and that he was her pathetic lapdog. He got very upset and Ava backed down.

Lucien and Ava carried on seeing each other, even more convinced of the necessity for cool-headedness. This latest upset proved to them that things could go wrong at any minute, that no one was too clever or too wise to screw up in love. But Ava couldn't do it any more. She was too irritated by the situation with Gertrude. When Gertrude rang Lucien's mobile at two in the morning – and he answered – Ava's blood started to fizz. When Gertrude referred to herself as a femme fatale, Ava practically choked. When Lucien and Gertrude next shared a hotel room, Ava considered buying a machete. Any hope of reason had vanished. Ava found herself suffering incessantly. When Lucien sent quick texts under the pub table she wanted to rip his nice hair out. When he drank out of the 'Gertrude is a babe' mug (still in his flat alongside a ton of other Gertrude memorabilia) she considered elbowing his tea into his lap. When he repeatedly commented on how clever Gertrude was for suggesting a cheap restaurant, she felt compelled to check his forehead for lobotomy scars. She started to think he was really stupid. Or that he was desperately insecure and could only feel okay if two women were fighting over him. Or that he was a hopeless Mummy's boy who couldn't cope with real relationships. She also began to wonder about herself. Why was she sticking with someone who made her so miserable? Was *he* being weird with *her*, or was she just a jealous freak? Was it really him who was making her unhappy, or was she somehow doing it to herself?

She tried to leave him again. This time he didn't seem at all upset, and that *really* annoyed her. She cried on and off for two days and then called an analyst.

Why, when her intentions had been so good, had she managed to end up miserable again?

Unhappily Ever After

A very large proportion of the world's most famous love stories end badly. *Dido and Aeneas* – how could he start packing up his ships without telling her? *Romeo and Juliet* – did she really have to wake up *just after* he took the poison? *Gone With the Wind* – how can he simply walk out like that? Jason and Medea, Anthony and Cleopatra, Charlotte and Werther, Anna Karenina and Vronsky, Emma Bovary and Rodolphe – all of these great love stories tend towards catastrophe. And that's before you get on to the morbidly fascinating romantic lives of Elizabeth Taylor and Richard Burton, Madonna and Guy Ritchie, maybe your parents and probably most of your friends. However delightful the first few months, days or minutes might be, it's highly likely that the rest will be unpleasant. While you might not actually have to stick yourself on a pyre, you may well find yourself having pyre-type fantasies about your 'loved one'.

But rather than simply saying that the beginning is nice and the ending is awful, it's usually the case that the ending was very much foreshadowed from the start. This may be a hoary old literary device, but it's also what you regularly see in day-to-day life. It's not uncommon for people to say, after ten years of marriage, 'I could tell he was a moany, selfish bastard within ten minutes of meeting him. Why the hell didn't I take it seriously back then?' When Dido met Aeneas she knew he was just passing through. It was plain to all concerned that Romeo and Juliet were heading for trouble. Rhett Butler had his first proper encounter with Scarlett O'Hara after popping out from behind the sofa having just overheard her declaring her love to Ashley. You could say that they all knew precisely what they were letting themselves in for.

But why would people *choose* to be miserable? And why is love such an effective means of achieving this aim?

In the early part of the nineteenth century, Arthur Schopenhauer came up with an explanation of why people fall in love. In his supplement to the fourth book of *The World as Will and Representation* he outlined what he saw as 'The Metaphysics of Sexual Love'. Romantic nonsense – consisting of all the 'exuberant feelings and immaterial soap bubbles' – grows out of the most serious of all human endeavours. He explains:

> The ultimate aim of all love affairs, whether played in sock
> or in buskin, is actually more important than all other
> aims in man's life; and therefore it is quite worthy of the
> profound seriousness with which everyone pursues it.
> What is decided by it is nothing less than the *composition*
> *of the next generation*.

How people come together is a matter of great interest to us because it concerns the continuation of the species. It's not simply that people have to mate, but that they have to produce '[t]he *dramatis personae* who will appear when [they] have retired from the scene'. They have to conjure up the best possible cast they can manage. Any faults they have may be ironed out of future generations if they can only find the right partner. The point of one's love object is to complement or counterbalance one's own imperfections. These imperfections may be physical or psychological – and the loved one may be quite imperfect too. The decisive factor is whether their imperfections promise to offset your own, and to result in new, improved individuals. Of course this idea may comfort you personally – 'My clever, pretty children will inherit the earth!' – but it's mainly good news for the species. As Schopenhauer sees it, the will of the individual is put at the service of the will of the species. You won't be around to see your grandchildren's marvellous grandchildren. What does it *really* matter to you what kind of people inhabit the future? The only entity that truly stands to benefit from your choice of sex-partner is the human race. And this is why love arrives with such a sense of urgency, even desperation. It's not just about you, it's about something much, much bigger acting through you. This is also what gives love its capacity to override obstacles. Who cares if she's a Capulet and you're a Montague? If, from a species-continuing point of view, she's perfect then you're just going to have to break a few social conventions. This is easier said than done, however, and may be quite cataclysmic for the individual. Schopenhauer describes a man in love thus:

> He strives after [his loved one] so eagerly that, to attain this end, he often, in defiance of all reason, sacrifices his own happiness in life by a foolish marriage, by love affairs that cost him his fortune, his honour, and his life, even by crimes such as adultery or rape; all merely in order to serve the species in the most appropriate way, in accordance

with the will of nature that is everywhere supreme,

although at the expense of the individual.

Because the concerns of the species are more important than the well-being of the individual, people may very often find themselves hitched to people they can't stand – or whom they feel passionate about but who nonetheless ruin their lives for other reasons. Schopenhauer was writing at a time shortly before Darwin's theory of evolution had begun to explain things like sexual selection. But his ideas about romantic choice fit perfectly well with later scientific theories. While he may have got some of the basic facts wrong – for instance, his idea that character is inherited from the father, intellect from the mother – he was ahead of his time in believing that the species may be hatching plans of which the individual has no inkling. One scientific view is that people sniff out appropriate partners, inadvertently screening each other's pheromones in search of a good biological match. If you find yourself suddenly drawn to someone who really isn't your type this is apparently because, between you, you have just the right DNA cocktail necessary to breed successfully. Any baby you had with this unappealing specimen would, in theory, have all four limbs, regular features and no genetically inherited diseases. The only problem is that the two of you might end up wanting to kill each other.

Thanks to his ideas about the will of the species, Schopenhauer is pretty scathing about arranged marriage. He says that love matches support the interests of the species, while arranged marriages privilege the here and now. While love matches are made with future generations in mind, arranged marriages are all about maintaining wealth and position in the present. 'In consequence of all this,' he tells us, 'it seems as if, in making a marriage, either the individual or the interest of the species must come off badly.' Neither romantic nor arranged marriages result in greater happiness – just because the social order has been maintained, there's no need to believe that spouses chosen by relatives will be any easier to live with. Arranged marriage simply attempts to stand in the way of our species' best interests.

Current anthropological work – perhaps done in the light of Jankowiak's suggestion that you need to look at what people *actually* do, rather than at what their society advises them to do – suggests that the will of the species may not be so easy to cheat. Recently, anthropologists have made studies of the realities of people's love lives in cultures where arranged marriage is practised. Divorce and infidelity turn out to be extremely common among people who don't choose their own spouses. From Kanuri Muslims in Nigeria to the !Kung Bushmen of the Kalahari, first marriages – which are always arranged – frequently end in divorce after less than a year, leaving each partner free to choose their next mate themselves.

So it appears that affairs and multiple divorces are far from simply being a result of capitalist individualism. In her book *Anatomy of Love*, Helen Fisher tells the story of Nisa, a !Kung woman who grew up watching her parents openly having sex with each other, as well as with other partners. When she was about sixteen Nisa's parents chose a husband for her. Despite having 'played at sex' with other children while she was growing up, she was inexperienced. As was the custom among the !Kung, an older woman stayed with her on her wedding night, ostensibly to show her the ropes. The woman, however, took the idea of teaching by example a bit too literally and spent the night having sex with Nisa's husband and nudging poor Nisa out of the bed. After only a few days of this, Nisa left. Next she was married to a second man who walked out after a few months because she wouldn't have sex with him. Finally, she married for love and it all went well, although she soon found herself having lots of affairs. She had children, presumably with both husband and lovers, and then her husband suddenly dropped dead. Nisa got on with being a single mum – and with having three boyfriends. One of the boyfriends finally pressed her into marriage, so they got hitched and drove each other mad; he had a massive sexual appetite and didn't like her seeing other men. Eventually they separated and she married a fifth time – and was still married to this husband when the interview took place. She continued to have a number of lovers, including her first teenage crush. In other words, she had a very interesting love life, which doesn't appear to have been curtailed for a minute by the practice of arranged marriage. (And she certainly didn't need to have a credit card or be surrounded by advertising in order to be sexually jumpy.) So, you could say that the will of the species has a tendency to win out over the wills of a small number of individuals – and that your parents or co-villagers are unlikely to be able to gang up and get the better of it.

♥

The advantage of Schopenhauer's theory over many contemporary theories of attraction is that it makes a space for the strangeness of particular instances of fancying. It's common these days to hear that people of equal attractiveness pair up. This idea is known as the 'matching hypothesis' and was put forward by Erving Goffman in 1952. Factors such as beauty, intelligence and wealth apparently combine to designate a person's social desirability (although beauty appears to hold the most sway for both men and women). This is all very well, but it assumes that everyone is pretty much agreed on who's attractive and who isn't. According to this theory, people simply try to bag the most generically appealing partner they can get their hands on. While of course it's likely to be true that more people have sexual fantasies about Johnny Depp than about Bill Gates, it's also true that beautiful, clever women sometimes date ugly, stupid men (who also have no money). And likewise with intelligent, handsome men and pinch-faced, witless women. Schopenhauer's theory is more subtle than Goffman's in that it has something to say about the mystifying nature of so many people's romantic choices. While Schopenhauer, like Goffman, believed that 'in the first place everyone will decidedly prefer and ardently desire the most beautiful individuals', there is a kind of two-tier system whereby people may also choose according to particular brands of faultiness. 'In the second place,' he tells us, '…he will find beautiful those imperfections that are the opposite of his own.' In other words, shy people may find themselves attracted to someone loud and garrulous, and an unusually short man may be irresistibly drawn to an ungainly giantess. 'A man specially selects for sexual satisfaction a woman with qualities that appeal to him individually.' As some people's self-diagnosed faults are often invisible to the external observer – a pathetic over-friendliness (no, actually you just seem nice), a tendency towards melancholy (a winsome glimmer of sadness) – it can be hard to see why they've picked such a hostile or hopelessly Pollyanna-ish partner. And, once the species has achieved its aim – or conclusively failed to achieve it – the couple will join the rest of us in wondering how they could have made such an unworkable choice.

The Displeasure Principle

If Schopenhauer's theory of love is a little bit grim, a century later Freud takes up a similar idea and makes it even worse. In his essay *Beyond the Pleasure Principle*, he discusses Weismann's germ plasm theory. This could be said to be a slightly more scientific version of Schopenhauer's notion of the will of the species. Weismann posited the existence of a germ plasm that could pass on hereditary characteristics from parent to child. (Something like DNA, although there were no means of proving its existence at the time.) The body was merely the soma that temporarily housed the germ plasm. People had sex in order to sustain the existence of the germ. This germ was not unlike Voldemort in the first book of Harry Potter, clinging to the back of Professor Quirrel's head in order to leech off his life force. And, like Voldemort, the germ plasm could make people act against their best interests.

The 'pleasure principle' refers to the idea that all living beings want to avoid pain and suffering. If something bugs them, be they a tree or a hippopotamus, they will do what they can to annul the irritant. The organism is driven by the wish to return to a previous state of comfort. If something burns you, you move away. If it's cold, you cover yourself. If you live on a fucked-up, scary planet full of dangerous creatures and freak natural occurrences, you develop opposable thumbs, walk upright, invent weapons and industrialized farming systems, and do whatever else you can think of to maintain a peaceful, womb-like existence. Of course it never quite works – another threat to your couch-potato-ness always comes along and forces you to do something. And so life on earth evolves.

According to Freud, life itself is a bizarre accident, an unlikely chemical occurrence. He conjures up an image of the earliest life-forms, living only briefly before returning to their original, inanimate state. Over millions of years, the gap between coming into existence and dying has been drastically extended. Some trees can live for a number of millennia. Icelandic scientists recently discovered a 400-year-old clam. (What's all this got to do with Elizabeth Taylor? We'll get there!) As Freud puts it: 'These circuitous paths to death...would thus present us today with the picture of the phenomena of life.' Life as we live it is just a complicated detour on the way to death. And one of the things that necessitates this detour is sex. The organism has to ensure its survival at least long enough to develop the appropriate sexual organs (the stamens of a flower, the ovaries of a mammal), find a mate, cross-pollinate – or whatever it is your particular species gets up to – and perhaps stick around long enough to bring up the offspring too. And this set of imperatives brings with it a second set – i.e. the necessity to stay able-bodied and disease-free until you've fulfilled your duty to propagate.

Of course human beings have evolved in such a way that the detour has become all-absorbing and need no longer involve breeding. In fact certain elements of the human detour seem to go very much against the easy possibility of making babies. For a start there is the fact that the apparatus we've built to stave off death is so elaborate and fascinating that we may simply be sidetracked by it, devoting our lives to, say, architecture or finding a cure for AIDS. Plus there's the fact that, in the name of this social apparatus, we've 'educated' sexuality to a point where it's very difficult for many people to enjoy it, or even to engage with it. Which is where Freud's theory becomes much darker than Schopenhauer's. Not only are we obliged by the germ plasm to have sex with people who may turn out to make us unhappy, but our sexuality has been warped by civilization to such a degree that it can actually make us ill – even before we are confronted by a hellish life with a rotten partner. Perhaps we can't bear to behave sexually at all. Perhaps we have fantasies that seem to have no place in a love relationship. Perhaps we are only attracted to people who are horrible to us, or who can't give us what we want. While this may appear to us to be simple bad luck – 'I thought she was so nice, but she turned out to be yet another psychotic bitch' – Freud would say it was actually the result of a deep-rooted and rather sinister compulsion to repeat. It's not simply that we are attracted to someone for a limited set of reasons, and then have to put up with all the bits that weren't covered by the attraction. Freud's really depressing idea is that we are actively seeking partners who can upset us in very particular (and familiar) ways.

The question is why we repeat the things we claim not to enjoy. The two possibilities are that either we *do* actually get some enjoyment from 'unfortunate' events, or that we are repeating something that went wrong last time in the hope of altering or mastering it (a bit like a two-year-old stacking building blocks and experiencing simultaneous joy and fury each time the stack crashes to the ground and has to be resurrected).

According to Freud we may be doing both. On the one hand we can get unconscious satisfaction from all sorts of peculiar things. We might get a kick out of having it proven, yet again, that we are useless wretches. It's not uncommon to get an enormous thrill out of wallowing in glorious self-pity. Perhaps we secretly enjoy acting out scenarios where other people are vile and beastly while we are snowy white. On the other hand, we may walk into situations that have floored us in the past in the hope that, this time, it will all be different. Perhaps not so much that we'll actually manage to alter the outcome – that a cold, forbidding father figure will suddenly turn around and love us madly (à *la* Mills and Boon) – but that we'll somehow get a buzz out of being treated with cool indifference because we *chose* it. Every little glimmer of affection will seem to us a great victory. And the frosty bits in between will be the perfectly painful counterpoint to the little flashes of victory. We vacillate between success and failure – each time the tower crashes we are disappointed, yet also somehow excited at the prospect of having another go. Misery can be so invigorating.

Which brings us back to Ava and Lucien…

Company and Crowds

Ava turned up at her analyst's office week after week. She told her shrink how irritating Gertrude was, how emotionally inarticulate her boyfriend was and what an idiot she was herself. She also went on at length about the unique awfulness of her own family relations. The analyst listened patiently, asking the odd question, trying to piece together the information in order to understand why this woman chose to stay in a relationship that apparently gave her so much cause for complaint. What kinds of satisfaction was she getting?

Ava described a family set-up in which three women competed for the affection and attention of one man. She felt she had lost out both to her mother and to her sister — that she was the one the father showed least interest in. With respect to her mother, she admitted defeat. But she developed a very rivalrous relationship with her sister, as if she continued to hold out hopes that this might be a battle she could win. As far as she could tell, she made very little progress and her sister remained much closer to their father throughout their lives.

Ava's parents were proper products of the 1960s and, like Nisa, she'd regularly witnessed their sexual activities first hand. As a teenager she often had to avert her eyes as she went into their bedroom for her lunch money before school. Up to the age of sixteen she was prudish and terrified of boys, but after that she was rarely without a boyfriend, sometimes going out with two or three simultaneously.

Over the years she developed all sorts of strategies in the hope of making herself interesting to men – nice clothes, friendliness, cooking, a reasonable grip on current affairs. Sometimes she took it a bit far, working in a hostess bar where she conned men into paying for bottle after bottle of overpriced champagne in return for the pleasure of her company. When men fell for her tricks too easily, she lost respect for them; if they were fooled by her semblance-of-a-woman act, then they were obviously stupid. Only if a man failed to be charmed by her performance was he worth the effort.

Her first marriage had provided her with a husband whose attention she could never quite get. He always seemed to have more pressing things to do than spend time with her. After a while it proved just *too* unsatisfying, so she started to have affairs. In this way she could show him that she didn't need his attention, simultaneously punishing him and puffing up her own fragile sense of self-worth. Eventually she left him for one of her lovers, whom she then married. This second husband seemed like a good antidote to the first. He was interested in every little thing about her. If she wore a new skirt he went mad, assuming she must be trying to attract the attention of someone else. If she put on make-up, she certainly had designs on another man. If he saw her car parked in an unusual place it was because she was sleeping with the inhabitant of the nearest house. This might have been great, but he counterbalanced these observations with equally microscopic examinations of her flaws – she had a stray hair on her chin, a white one on her head, her teeth were a little discoloured and she had cellulite on her thighs. For every time he boosted her ego with his suspicion that she had a flock of admirers, he found another two opportunities to remind her that she wasn't actually that great. After four years of this, the insults started to outweigh the compliments a little too heavily. It got to her. She began to believe that she couldn't ever leave him because she was obviously too hideous to ever find someone else. But somehow she did. And, after a few brief affairs, she met Lucien.

In retrospect she wondered whether, during the first minutes of their meeting, she hadn't seen that he was perfectly designed to upset her. He was nice but not at all flirty, much more inter-ested in asking serious questions about her work than in telling her she had a pretty dress on. So it would therefore be possible to like him. But he also came with a built-in rival. If she got together with him she could mess around trying to get his atten-tion, breaking down his coolness, etc., at the same time as re-enacting a family battle. Maybe this time she'd even win. It was too perfect.

The problem with these too-perfect scenarios is that it's unusual to find two people whose pathologies are perfectly suited. In this case, it's unclear what Lucien's reason for choosing Ava was – perhaps she reminded him of his sister (Gertrude's arch enemy) or maybe it was something else altogether. What-ever it was, he'd very likely spotted *something* about her that promised to open up his psychic wounds just so. So the pair found themselves acting out roles from two entirely different dramas, each perplexed by the other's actions and reactions.

As Freud conceptualizes it, we begin our sexual researches pretty much the minute we are born, but have it gradually knocked out of us. We are soon taught that we aren't allowed to try to get erotic enjoyment from our own or other people's bodies. We start looking for other, more socially acceptable ways to get satisfaction. So we ride go-carts and learn to play the trumpet. Children, who are inclined to love passionately, experience the limits placed on their sexual urges as rejections. As a child grows up, Freud tells us, the 'lessening amount of affection he receives, the increasing demands of education, hard words and an occasional punishment – these show him at last the full extent to which he has been *scorned*'. And this isn't to mention the unfortunate events that can occur in the other direction – unwanted sexual advances from adults, or even just low-level, invasive attention. When we reach an age at which we are finally allowed to act on our erotic wishes, it turns out that these early experiences have a left a mark on us. We can't start doing whatever we like with no unfortunate consequences. We might still be rejected, or find ourselves suddenly at the mercy of someone else's overwhelming desires. We may feel guilty about what we want, having been told early on that it was somehow unacceptable. After such a shaky and disappointing run-up it turns out not to be so easy to launch into love and sex with abandon. We invariably find out that we are already a little bit screwed.

♥

Ava's analyst listened and listened, and finally presented her with the idea that she may have an unconscious fascination with the idea of seeing her lover in bed with someone else. Ava was shocked. Did she? She certainly didn't get a *conscious* thrill out of the thought of Lucien and Gertrude together – in fact she found it quite repulsive. But she had to admit there was a certain *charge* around the whole idea. That the very particular rage and misery she felt when they shared a room was somehow exhilarating – it had much the same flavour as the fury she felt at her parents for flouting their sexuality in front of her. It wasn't pleasure in any normal sense – she *hated* it – but then again it was bizarrely compelling. Why did these two couples need to inflict their coupleness on her, put it on show? She didn't want to know about Lucien and Gertrude in the same way that she didn't want to know about her mum and dad. Let's call it the repressed way – deep down she was shamefully, desperately curious about both. But her filthy interest was *all their fault*. They were the ones who'd roused her curiosity, shown her too much, dangled things in front of her. She hadn't asked them to do it. (And on the subject of dangly bits, her parents had always walked around naked when she was a child. She'd never found it natural and by the by, but had always had the sense that they were actively *exposing* themselves. In her mind, Lucien and Gertrude were somehow doing the same thing.)

Ava definitely enjoyed the feeling of self-righteousness it all gave her. Why did the bastards have to make her watch? Did they need external observers in order to believe in their own relationship? She also liked the fact that it licensed her to fight with Lucien, rather than going around pretending to be reasonable and mature. She noticed she got a peculiar kick out of noting Gertrude's flaws and developing private, Bette Davis-style insults to fit them. Unlike with her parents and sister, in this situation she could ask questions, make a fuss and even expect answers. All in all, it began to seem possible that she'd stumbled across a form of unhappiness that suited her very well.

Cry, Baby

Freud's theory seems to have a lot going for it, but does it have any bearing on reality? Do we *really* choose people who allow us to repeat our infantile sexual traumas, the partners most likely to drop us back into an all too familiar hell? Or will we just build a hell with whomsoever we happen to stumble across? It can be hard to tell because it's impossible to disentangle knowledge gained with hindsight from what you knew at the time. Perhaps a certain look or gesture really did mean nothing to you when you first saw it, but then you were able to imbue it with significance later. While you might now have the sense that all the things you hate about your partner were visible right from the off, perhaps this is an illusion. Or, then again, perhaps the illusion was the initial not-knowing, the repressions and defences that temporarily tricked you into imagining that everything was going to be just great.

Towards the end of *Beyond the Pleasure Principle*, Freud himself wrote: 'I am not convinced myself and ... I do not seek to persuade other people of the truth of [these hypotheses].' His theory is so poetic, paradoxical and impervious to empirical testing that it's impossible to know quite how to take it. You can ask yourself, your friends and your acquaintances about their experiences. (I recently asked the plumber, and I always ask taxi drivers.) You can read fiction or biographies. Apparently Richard Burton's first words to Elizabeth Taylor on the set of *Cleopatra* were: 'You're much too fat, luv. But I admit you do have a pretty little face.' If that isn't a man who can upset you, I don't know what is. And he was a drinker, like her father. She'd come across him a few times before and wondered, 'Does that man ever shut up?' In short, the course of this particular love was never going to run smooth. Once, when Elizabeth wondered aloud whether she and Richard might marry, he responded, 'If we don't kill each other first.' Her riposte to this was, 'But what a way to go, darling. What a way to go.' Elizabeth Taylor, with her eight marriages, is a kind of standard-bearer for the compulsion to repeat. Still, on her own, she can hardly be called on to prop up Freudian theory.

So how else might we explain why unhappiness seems to be a necessary component of romance? Romantic movies have long been referred to as 'weepies' and 'tear-jerkers'. They've always been popular box-office fodder. If you can make people cry, you're rich. There's clearly something enjoyable about romantic failures and disappointments. Especially other people's. Plus there's the fact that crying itself is somehow pleasurable. There are the tears of happiness that come when people manage to sort their problems out and be nice to each other, but mainly there's the beautiful sadness that comes from seeing people dying, being rejected, separated by circumstance or giving each other up for the greater good. When people in films weep, they tend to look rather lovely. Ovid, in *The Art of Love*, recommends it to both men and women. Men should do it because it makes them appear sensitive and poetic. Women too might find themselves surprisingly alluring when they are in full flow:

… Could chained Andromeda have dreamt
She would attract a lover, blubbering, unkempt?
Yet we know that when a man
Dies and the widow's plan
Is to find a new one, a parade of funeral feeling —
Dishevelled hair, abandoned sobs — is quite appealing.

Crying is still very little understood. Human beings are thought to be the only species that do it. Lots of other mammals have tear ducts in order to keep their eyeballs permanently damp, but we are the only ones who leak and sob for emotional reasons (although there is apparently a vague question mark over the sentimental lives of elephants, camels and gorillas). Some biologists believe we cry in order to rid our bodies of certain hormones — the chemical make-up of emotional tears is very different to that of the toe-stubbing, onion-chopping variety. The idea is that we are purging ourselves of the chemicals that have made us feel so worked up in the first place. Another theory is that we cry, thereby releasing a load of hormones into our bloodstream, in order to make ourselves feel even *more* unbalanced. When we are all cried out, we return to our average hormonal state and it's as if everything's suddenly much better. In other words, crying makes us feel super-weird so we can be relieved afterwards, giving us the strange illusion that external matters have improved. This is basically a biochemical retelling of Aristotle's theory of catharsis; when we cry (over either a fictitious drama or the drama of our own existence) we manage to work off some emotion, to purify ourselves in order that we can then get on with feeling moderately normal and happy.

A third explanation for crying (which needn't contradict the other two) is that it's a very particular form of communication designed to cause other people to help us. Babies cry in the hope that they can persuade their carers to do stuff for them. Adults may cry to prove the strength of their feelings, to show other people how hurt they are or how much something matters to them. It's as if crying is there as an alternative to words – a special thing one can call on when speaking isn't enough. Instead of simply *explaining* to someone that what they are doing is upsetting you, you can *show* them how they are affecting you by blubbering into a hankie. Dido, when she discovers that Aeneas is packing up to leave, tearfully asks him to reconsider, saying, 'I beg you, by these tears, by the pledge you gave me with your own right hand.' When he apologizes and tells her that, unfortunately, he really does have to go off and found Rome, she is appalled. 'He did not sigh when he saw me weep,' she says. 'He did not even turn to look at me. Was he overcome and brought to tears? Had he any pity for the woman who loves him?' It's unthinkable to Dido, much as it is to Scarlett O'Hara at the end of *Gone With the Wind*, that her loved one can be so unmoved by her sobbing.

It comes across as almost unimaginably cruel. And this is the problem with tears. On the one hand there is something inadvertent about them, something that can't be helped. But on the other hand they can be a manipulative device, a really good way of getting what you want. When Aeneas and Rhett Butler manage to stick to their original plans in the face of their women's weeping it's hard to know whether to be horrified or impressed. (At least Aeneas seems to give a damn – just not quite enough of one to actually stick around.)

People have always tried to draw up a distinction between real crying and crocodile tears; Dido actually means it, but you have to watch out for Scarlett. For Roland Barthes, in *A Lover's Discourse*, *all* tears are suspect. 'I adapt my ways of weeping,' he tells us, 'to the kind of blackmail which, by my tears, I mean to exercise around me.' It's not that he's wilfully faking, just that tears inevitably contain this communicative dimension – a demand for something to be done. In other words, the lover, in crying, 'accepts rediscovering the *infant body*' (Barthes' italics). We cry over the actions and reactions of our loved ones like babies cry over their mothers; it's a very good way of generating a response. Thanks to the fact that crying is a physical reaction, something we could do before we learnt more sophisticated tricks, it carries with it an aura of authenticity. But this appearance of 'realness' is put at the service of signification. Tears say that, this time, you really, really mean it.

The idea of fake crying is something most of us find quite heinous. It's as if weeping is thought to be a bit sacred, and to fake it is a serious transgression. But what's so sacrosanct about a bit of salty water and a scrunched-up face? Why would Dido imagine that her tears should be serious enough to steer Aeneas away from his destiny? It appears that tears, like orgasms, are guarantors of some form of truth. They are a way of relating to others without the potential sophistry of language, a means of bypassing representations and accessing something real. And because of this they have a special power, which makes them a very good tool for people who like to get what they want. Scarlett O'Hara is shamelessly manipulative and uses tears like she uses smiles and off-the-shoulder dresses – as seductive ruses. At the very end of the film there's a bit of uncertainty as to whether she's for real this time. Maybe she is. And the idea that, for once, she's not bullshitting is enough to make the last scene properly moving. (Until she ruins everything and says, 'Tomorrow is another day.' Stupid!)

What's really amazing about tears and cinema is that the trick works *on the audience*; that we are moved by their fake crying enough that *we* can actually muster an authentic bodily reaction while sitting in the dark, perhaps even on our own. In spite of the fact that the figures on screen are just actors being paid, we care enough about them that their fate seems to matter to us. Is it possible that weepies provide us with a chemical experience – a hormone rush, followed by a lull – that tricks us into feeling better about our real lives (even if only temporarily)? Or could it be that the illnesses, accidents and disasters somehow keep the illusion of love afloat? As long as people are ripped apart by *something* then their interrupted happiness can remain as a kind of potent blank space. Real lives together are always going to be filled with frustration and shopping bills. Everyone knows that Romeo and Juliet would have got on each other's nerves after a month or two. Romantic tragedies are great because they hint at impossible futures in which love might not have been a disappointing mess. While we may think we are crying over Rhett's indifference, Romeo and Juliet's horrible families, or our own lover's lack of consideration, we may actually be lamenting the fact that love itself is never actually that great, that it's only the things that *don't* happen that can keep alive any semblance of an ideal. Perhaps Ava's annoyance with Lucien and Gertrude had as much to do with the fact that they were separated as with the idea that they were somehow still attached. They'd escaped. They no longer needed to deal with each other in the devastating context of a love relation. They could now have a cosy friendship in the comforting glow of what might have been but never was.

Perhaps you could even go so far as to say that, when we cry over a romantic tragedy, we are crying tears of *happiness* over the couple's misfortune; that anything's better than trying to live happily ever after. And maybe the reason we keep falling in love, in spite of our unhappy experiences and the gloomy statistics, is precisely *because* it will probably all end in tears.

3.

Crazy In Love

Why love drives us insane

♥　　♥

In which we meet Young Werther (amongst other nutty stalkers) and try to understand why love drives us mad

THERE IS ALWAYS SOME MADNESS IN LOVE. BUT
THERE IS ALSO ALWAYS SOME REASON IN MADNESS.

Friedrich Nietzsche

In 1970s Connecticut a young psychology professor called Dorothy Tennov decided that our vocabulary for describing romantic suffering was inadequate. Why was there no proper word to express that insane state at the beginning of a romance when hopping on a bus at two in the morning or spending two hundred pounds on a haircut seems like just the thing to do? There was 'infatuation', but it had derogatory overtones, seeming to carry the idea that it was a false emotion. There were 'crushes', which were necessarily immature and adolescent. Being 'in love', as opposed to 'loving', was an option, but this thing was different from love, wasn't it? If love was what you felt for your child, your stable partner, your parents, then this had nothing to do with it.

She started asking her students about their love lives. They told her lots of stories about missing whole terms' worth of study through mooning around and generally having a horrible time.

Tennov outlined her burgeoning research to a female friend who looked at her blankly and said she'd never felt anything of the sort. This was apparently a breakthrough moment. Here was a good friend, clearly not autistic. She had children, ex-husbands, boyfriends – she claimed to have experienced love. But she had never swooned and stammered and shredded flowers over it; she hadn't suffered a mad passion. By witnessing its non-appearance in someone she knew, Tennov became more convinced that there was a particular emotional state, quite distinct from love, which deserved study. She called it 'limerence' – for no reason other than that it seemed to her to sound right. If she could pin it down and define it then it promised to make sense of all sorts of things.

Out of this revelation came the book *Love and Limerence: The Experience of Being in Love* – a great wad of pages with the word 'limerence' appearing at least once on almost every one. By the end you almost start to believe in it. Apparently the writer Capellanus did, or at least he 'accepted its existence', in spite of living in the eleventh century. On the back it says, 'You'll be an eighties dropout if you don't read this book.' There is an aura around the publication that suggests this really is a big discovery; the fourth Copernican revolution. Wow, we've been going around for the last few millennia completely ignoring the elephant that is limerence! How come we've kidded ourselves all this time that it had anything to do with love? The Egyptians, the Greeks, the

Romans were all being silly. Not to mention the Elizabethans and Victorians. Limerence is a distinct emotion and if only people had cottoned on sooner then Cleopatra, Dido and Anne Boleyn might have lived to be old ladies.

You could be generous and say that it's really very hard to be an academic – you're supposed to keep producing original research at an unrealistic rate. Or you could say that coming up with neologisms to describe things that we already have perfectly arbitrary and inadequate words for, thank you, is one of the first signs of madness. The evangelical zeal with which Tennov promoted her word – firing off corrections if someone dared to define it slightly wrong on their website, for instance – suggests an unusual level of investment in it. You might even say that she loved it. Or was she just limerent over it?

Now that Tennov is no longer around to get annoyed about it, it may be safe to risk a definition. Limerence refers to the state in which one thinks constantly about the exciting person – or LO (limerent object), to use the jargon – and suffers terribly over the idea that one's feelings might not be returned. It's an amorous over-investment that demands reciprocation, and it comes with all sorts of hideous side-effects such as intrusive thoughts and a sense of all-round desperation.

In a reversal of the private game whereby one can drain all meaning from a word by repeating it over and over, it seems equally possible to invest a word with meaning by inserting it in a discourse, using it as much as possible and treating anyone who doesn't accept it as an idiot. There's no real reason *not* to call that painful initial rush of emotion 'limerence' – plenty of people give names to their addictions, manias and bad moods. But one has to accept that the name is an artifice. Of course the word 'love' is an arbitrary signifier too, but it's a signifier that's been doing a perfectly good job over a considerable period of time. In fact it's been working extremely hard, doing about ten jobs and getting rather exhausted in the process. This, of course, was Tennov's beef. She thought it was time we gave 'love' a break, delegated a few of its responsibilities.

Still, it seems that it wasn't just the quantity of work that she objected to, but also the nature of it. The interesting thing about limerence is that it is a concept that tries to clean up love. Tennov picks out all the other, nicer forms of love and attraction – friendship, familial love, sexual attraction and true love – and separates limerence from them. It's as if she wants to partition the madness off so that love can be nice again.

Tennov is sniffy about Freud, and it's easy to see why. Freud's huge and innovative contribution was to say precisely that all the different types of love are linked. A child is an erotic doll for the mother, a baby gets off on being cuddled, cleaned and watched, a father's tellings-off can produce intense sexual excitement, friendship relies on a repressed erotic component, etc. According-ing to Freud, it's the very over-stretchedness of the word 'love' that gives us an insight into the way the emotion is structured. A baby might very well be described as being limerent over its mother when it cries every time she leaves the room. A mother may suffer some kind of limerence when her child starts saying, 'Go away, I don't need you any more.' Of course you can switch the word limerence for love if you want to, but it can't cleanse your psyche of the unbearable history of your emotions. Tennov's project seems to involve purging adult love of any of its unacceptable links with infantile sexuality. She has little to say about the origins of limerence – not only is it a word without an etymology, it is also an emotion without roots. It just *is*. In short, her project to subtract madness from love is, in itself, a little bit nutty.

While it's all very well to point out that love can tip you over the limit – people have been pretty vocal on that point for the last few thousand years – the question is why. By what mechanisms might romantic attachment push otherwise reasonable people to think, feel and do unreasonable things? Of course it won't be possible to answer the question definitively – there are so many competing theories that the search for answers may drive you mad, if being in love hasn't got you already.

Before going into the psychology of mad love it might be useful to look at one or two literary cases of it in order to study the symptoms more carefully – and to ask whether there's really any difference between, say, Young Werther's relentless pursuit of Charlotte and the behaviour that we now call stalking. Maybe intense romantic love is fundamentally sick and twisted, and the most impressive thing about it is that anyone has ever managed to persuade us that it's somehow noble and beautiful.

The Stalking Cure

One of the nicest, and least falsely noble, contemporary books on love is Gregory Dart's *Unrequited Love: On Stalking and Being*

Stalked. It's the first-hand account of an English lecturer who finds himself being stalked by a young girl – a PhD student from another university. Because he is an academic his response is not to go to the police but to write an extended essay about the effects of the modern metropolis on our sentimental lives. This is actually *genuinely* noble of him, although I imagine the girl wasn't overly flattered by his portrayal of her. One of the many amazing things about his book is that it describes a chain of stalking whereby each lovestruck maniac infects his or her victim with the disease, much like a vampire. Lucy, the anti-heroine, tells Gregory in one of their first conversations that she is being harassed by a former friend, and bombarded with messages and invitations. She then proceeds to do precisely the same to Gregory, insulting him when he doesn't respond enthusiastically. Gregory is very upset by her constant invasive criticism and becomes a bit of an emotional recluse. When he finally manages to shake her off he goes through a kind of convalescent period, fearing he will never love again. He buys a load of self-help books on stalking, and contemplates Stendhal, Goethe, Dante and Poe. Then, out of the blue, he falls in love with a girl after a brief conversation at his gym and finds himself trawling the East End day after day, desperately hoping to bump into her. (Who knows whether she then went on to badger some other poor innocent, but my guess is probably not, as Gregory Dart's stalking was extremely polite, as befits a specialist in Romantic literature.)

So what was the strange effect that appeared to be passing through these people like an electric current through a wire?

Certainly each episode began with an act of kindness shown by the stalkee to the stalker. Gregory had spoken to Lucy at a conference where she'd been looking lost and lonely. The gym girl had smiled at Gregory and commented on his fitness without any prompting from him. They'd both gone out of their way to be nice. This is something you also often see in the more sinister cases of stalking reported in the newspapers. Tracey Morgan, who was aggressively stalked for years and who is largely responsible for the institution of tighter anti-stalking laws in Britain, made an effort to be kind to a neighbour and was thanked by years of silent phone calls, nasty letters and dog shit in inappropriate places. It seems that in some instances these small, benevolent gestures can produce enormous consequences – but presumably only if certain preconditions are in place. Whatever they may mean to the person performing them, they seem to mean a great deal more to the one on the receiving end – as if they perfectly answer to a particular need at a particular moment. Lucy's best friend had just died but she'd turned up at the conference anyway 'because that's what [her friend] would have wanted'. She's standing there feeling bereft and devastated and, as if from nowhere, a handsome man walks up to her, talks to her and buys her a drink. Her prayers have been answered. It must mean something. Whether or not he knows it yet, he's The One. It's as if he's walked into one of those leaf-covered, hole-in-the-ground-style traps – a space designated for someone to fall into.

Similarly, Gregory develops his crush at the moment he's begun to feel like love might not only be possible but necessary.

His solitude no longer signifies safety, but something sad and static. He needs to recover from his disturbing experience with Lucy by finding somebody to love. When the gym girl smiles at him she has no idea what she's done. She might as well have passed through an invisible laser whose broken beam triggers an impossibly complex mechanical reaction; she has imperceptibly set Gregory's romantic machinery in motion. She's answered a need in him *without being asked*. And it seems to be this not being asked that makes it all the more effective, gives it a 'naturalness' or inevitability that persuades the recipient that it means more than it does – or at least more than it was meant to. You haven't shoehorned them into your ludicrous world, they have wandered in of their own volition.

And this is perhaps where the madness kicks in. The other person has answered something in you so perfectly that it can seem that they have linked themselves to you, or even become a part of you. They've filled a hole in your psychic space, inserted an image where there used to be a blank. Without being invited, they've joined you, taking up a position in your psychic economy. On some level, they're yours already. And this madness isn't particular to stalkers – something like it could be said to happen in every case of romantic love. Chance has caused another person to fit your romantic bill. If you're lucky, you'll fit theirs too. But, perhaps more likely, you won't. You're not their type. They're already madly in love with someone else. They are a loner and can only get off on porn. Whatever. There's something almost purely mathematical about it; probability dictates that once in a while two people will feel that they need each other equally. Other than that it's all just wrong numbers.

Biological theories of love, while being very fascinating, don't seem to have much to say about the fact that a large percentage of attractions only go one way. If there is the idea that we like who we like because their pheromones tell us that they are our perfect genetic match and our babies will be healthy and strong, what about the fact that so often it's only one half of the pair who wants to exchange fluids? Is it because the other person is biologically unintuitive (and is that a genetic condition)? Is it because they are at different levels of the bio-hierarchy (the lover isn't as attractive as the beloved)? Or is it because, as we are 'civilized' beings – i.e. beings on an exceptionally complex route to death – biology is the least of our worries. We also have to consider education, money, class, levels of tidiness, favourite films and the amount of time it's appropriate to spend in Tesco. Not to mention the fact that the very idea of babies might make us puke. Or that we might be gay. Or both. The current scientific position on love smacks of Aristophanes' idea in Plato's *Symposium* that we are descended from globular creatures who were split in two by Zeus, and are therefore destined to search desperately for our other halves. (Although even this theory took gays and lesbians into account – many of the blobs were made from two same-sex halves. Only one third were heterosexual.) If we believe that our noses guide us towards a perfect genetic match, then we can sustain the illusion that there really is an immaculate partner for us – and that when we meet them it will be mutually satisfying.

Sturm und Drang

Goethe's Young Werther is the ultimate loved-up nutcase. He falls for someone engaged and pants around after her until she finally has to tell him to back off. The rejection is unbearable and he shoots himself in the head. Like most other stalking stories, *The Sorrows of Young Werther* gets going when the stalkee goes out of her way to be kind. Werther arrives in the village of Wahlheim, barely knowing anyone. At a party, Charlotte re-arranges things so that Werther can dance with her. The laser beam is broken, the puzzle piece fits, she's inserted herself into his psyche. It's clear to pretty much everyone that she likes him – but that doesn't mean she'll ditch Albert on his behalf. Werther can't give up on the idea that she is somehow *his* and finally comes up with the notion that it's impossible for Albert, Charlotte and himself to co-exist. He's not really the murderous type, so that leaves suicide.

When it was published in 1774, the story was an immediate hit, inducing Werther-Fever and supposedly prompting around two thousand unhappy lovers to blow their brains out. (Considerably worse than any heavy metal record.) It is one of the most celebrated products of the *sturm und drang* movement at the end of the eighteenth century – an artistic movement which, like emo, explores and celebrates being emotionally fucked up. If the Enlightenment had gone all out to persuade people that it was possible to choose to be sensible and good – that reason could override anything – then books like *The Sorrows of Young Werther* sought to remind everyone that it's not really like that. And people seemed to like being told – or at least to find it a relief after all that self-deluding uprightness.

Certainly books like Goethe's can be comforting when you're in the thick of it. They seem to normalize the madness, making it less incomprehensible. But we could equally say that they invent an ideal of love that then has to be perpetuated. Is Goethe telling it like it is? Or is he making it look like he wants it to? And if he wants it to look like that, why are we so ready to go along with him? If love is a delusion that covers up the fundamental impossibility of gaining satisfaction from another person, then are books like *Young Werther* just there to help us shape the fallacy? To give us a set of thoughts and actions that ostensibly constitute 'love'? Or do they help us by giving us a space to make sense of the unbearable things we feel?

Pleased to Meat You

To be madly in love is to be a kind of psychic cannibal. There is a wish to incorporate the other person. You want to include them in your life, be near them, spend time with them. You want to consume them. The idea that they might have no interest in inserting themselves into your scheme of things is unbearable. (I always feel for real cannibals, particularly the ones who've been polite enough to get consent from their 'victims'. The only thing I can't bear is when they add other ingredients to the meal – garlic or a dash of white wine. To want to eat someone is quite forgivable, but to flavour their flesh like any old meat seems disrespectful. I'm sure the famous German cannibal, Armin Miewes, would have got a shorter sentence if he hadn't flambéed his friend's penis.) A large part of the madness of love seems to spring from this confusion about what's you and what's them. If love is triggered when someone fits into the space in your mental puzzle, it can be very confusing when they don't see it that way. Imagine doing a thousand-piece jigsaw over the course of a long and wet weekend. It's quite boring but you persist. You finally get to the last bit. It fits perfectly in the wiggly hole and the patterns appear to you to match the general picture. After all that hard work it's strangely satisfying. Now imagine someone telling you that this isn't in fact the correct piece. It's actually part of another puzzle that just happens to look right by chance. They take the piece away and you are left with an irritating blank. And then, just to really annoy and upset you, they show you how it fits much better into another jigsaw. (What kind of imaginary friends do *you* have?)

Even when it ostensibly works – you like them, they like you – insanity isn't necessarily avoided. The next problem is accessing the thing you seem to like about them, dealing with the bits of them that don't quite fit the designated space, and generally coping with the fact that getting what you want is never quite as simple as you'd hoped it might be. If you're lucky there will be some external obstacle to justify your craziness. Maybe they are married or live in another country. If you are unlucky they will be entirely yours and you will be unable to justify your derangement. During brief spells of separation you find yourself writing poems or lengthy emails. You think about your love object at every opportunity, becoming temporarily crap at your job. Even when they are there you become tormented by the idea that they might leave you, or that they don't love you enough. In short, you have to face the awful fact that they are another person with an independent will and private thoughts. Yes, whatever nice things they say, however often they seem to want to see you, they might well abandon you eventually. (Especially if you insist on moping around, asking them what they're thinking the minute they go quiet and trying to get them to explain what it is they like about you.)

In a sense it needn't matter too much whether you believe romantic-object choice is down to your DNA or whether you believe in the Freudian notion of searching for facsimiles of your early care-givers; in either case you face the same problem. Having singled the person out as special you are then on a collision course to finding out exactly why things aren't quite as they seem. Both scientists and psychoanalysts largely agree that love is there in order to temporarily blind us to the horrors of proximity. Evolutionary biologists will tell you that the neurochemical explosions that produce the experience we call love are necessary to stop us seeing other people as a threat – for at least as long as it takes us to breed. It works exactly like a tab of ecstasy. As soon as the drugs wear off we may well have to face the fact that we hate their tweed jackets and the way they think Ian McEwan is a good writer. (That they are a serious threat to our sense of good taste.) Equally, psychoanalysts – particularly Lacanians – are prone to explain love as a production that stops us seeing that there is no real or inevitable bond between ourselves and the other person; we are just using them to sate our drives and prop up our fantasies.

In either case love just *is* mad. It's a bit like a hallucination; what comes from the inside appears to come at us from the outside; something *in them* is supposedly making us love them. Our love isn't our fault – they've made us do it by being so intrinsically loveable. Love also shares features with obsessional disorders in the sense that certain thoughts and actions have to be repeated over and over as if we are trying to master an impossibility, or to think about one thing in order to block out something else. (In that sense the shrinks and the scientists also overlap – brain scans of lovers in a state of infatuation apparently match brain scans of obsessive-compulsive disorder sufferers.) Perhaps if we take a break from imagining the joys of kissing, our minds will stray to the absolute ludicrousness of the entire enterprise. And, here again, love shares features with delusional illness – the symptom is in fact an attempt at cure. A psychotic can subdue an unbearable sense of boundless pain and chaos by conjuring up an agency whose aim is to torment them – anything from the FBI to aliens. The delusional idea is a stab at limiting the unbelievable horror of *being* by giving it a valid cause. You still feel wildly distraught, but at least now you know it's because the government is watching you. Anyone would feel the same in your shoes. In love, perhaps, a similar thing is happening. All the painfully pleasurable thoughts about the loved one need to be turned over and over so that we *don't* have to think about the gigantic lunacy of what we are doing. The delightful madness of love – 'They're so marvellous I mustn't take my mind off them for a second!' – is a barrier against the more worrying insanity of attempting to link bodies, circumstances, destinies with another independent being.

The Greatest Thing You'll Ever Learn

Freud was originally a neurologist and looked forward to a time when advances in technology would make it possible to explain some of the phenomena he observed in his clinic. Although that time may have arrived, there's huge reluctance from both camps to see it that way. The neurobiologists are happy to view love as a chemical reaction, seeing Freud's work as outdated and disproven. The shrinks often tend to see the scientists as blinkered drones working within a very limited set of ideas about the mind. Given that neither camp has very good grounds for saying that the other is simply wrong, they might be better off listening to each other for a minute and seeing what they can come up with.

One problem with taking current biochemical views on their own is that they have so little to say about love that doesn't lead to babies. And that doesn't just mean gay people or people who fool biology by using contraceptives. It also means women who fall madly in love in their mid-seventies and people who lust after TV personalities they've never remotely had the chance to sniff. Alternately, the problem with ignoring the neurobiologists is that they're obviously onto something and if you deny it you look a bit like a flat-earther. Neurotransmitters are not going to go away.

So, by taking both brain chemicals and psycho-sexual development into account, what can we say about love and madness? On the one hand, yes, an influx of dopamine and norepinephrine and a drop in serotonin might make you feel a bit funny, but what made the chemicals kick in in the first place? If it isn't *just* a whiff of the right brand of pheromone, then what is it? How come it can also be triggered by a photograph, an email or a voice at the end of a phone? Freud pointed to the fact that human beings, by standing on two legs and wearing clothes and perfumes, have shifted a long way from our predecessors in that we have very little chance to smell each other's privates. Over the last few million years we have developed all sorts of funny ways of choosing mates. The structure of human societies means that one's place in the hierarchy has nothing to do with strength or looks – you can be ugly and puny as hell, but if you're rich that'll do nicely. And anyhow you can change your genetic destiny with surgery, meaning that no one will know you're a bad bet on the beautiful baby front. We are less explicitly interested in smelling people than in finding out what music they like, or whether they enjoy hiking. We are very problematic animals.

Human infants are born completely helpless, so have to be looked after for years. On the neurobiological front this means that mothers and, to a lesser extent, fathers have to stay pumped full of love chemicals in order to tolerate the inconvenience. The neurotransmitters released in nursing mothers – and in the babies they are caring for – are the very ones that are released in the experience of sexual love. So, in a purely chemical sense

Freud was right – infantile love and adult love can't be clearly distinguished. (On the other hand, Tennov was onto something in that dopamine, norepinephrine, and serotonin are generally released in larger doses during the initial phase of attraction, while oxytocin and vasopressin are more important in the formation of lasting relationships. Mad love and long-term love involve subtly different chemical cocktails.)

One effect of our prolonged period of helplessness in infancy is that we get plenty of chances to get excited by this person, ignored by that person, mistreated by the other one. We learn that we like this; we don't like that; if we do this, that will happen. We build up an internal fact-file on the best means of getting satisfaction from other people. To put it more delicately, we try to work out how to love and be loved. And this impressive amount of information is what we then use in our attempts to bring about the same results later. Of course some of the data may be a little unreliable – redheaded people are cuddly, men with beards are scary and people seem to like it when we sing – but we can't help mistakenly drawing on it in our quest for affection.

For a baby, reciprocity is key. There are lots of things you need and want, but you have absolutely no means of getting them on your own. At first you can just howl and people will take care of you. (Some of us never drop this tactic and are still banking on it well into our thirties and forties.) But after a while you have to get a bit more crafty. You learn to ask nicely, to charm people, to give them what they want in return for what you want – all the tricks that set you up for life in a civilized society. And, as we've said, crying may still play a part in this. Of course you still have tantrums when it gets too difficult to be nice. And that can be quite often because the extent to which your happiness depends on other people is intolerable. Basically, the whole game sucks. And the promise is that when you grow up you won't have to do it any more. You'll go and get your own drinks, your own food, your own clothes. You won't have to depend on anyone for anything. The only problem is that it turns out not to be that way. It wasn't just the clothes and the drinks you wanted, it was the proof of love that came with them. You can buy yourself as many fancy meals as you like but it doesn't mean much if you have to eat them alone.

So you're back to square one – the unbearable frustration of reciprocal love. No wonder it makes you feel like screaming and crying. That's how it all began. Your life depended on your ability to get people to respond to you. It can feel like it still does. Imagine taking a drug that sent you right back to being a baby again. Only this time you are a baby in an adult's body with an adult's responsibilities. It's shameful. You're supposed to be over it by now.

If Love is Mad, Writing About It is Even Madder

If, as neurobiologists tell us, love is made from oxytocin circulating in the brain, how does that fit with a sudden falling away of love when the person you're with does something that puts you off them? Was there a chemical drop, which caused you to stop loving them? Or did your stopping loving them cause a chemical drop? Just speaking logically, love can't be wholly reduced to the chemicals in you responding to the chemicals in your partner. It's more complex than that. It's not simply that the body affects the mind, but also that the mind affects the body. If you are pheromonally attracted to someone you are going to have to deal with it somehow. If some unnerving force in your body is causing you to be drawn to someone else's body then you will have to find a way to mediate the relation. You can't simply leave your bodies to get on with it – or you can, and that's a very common fantasy, but it's actually probably harder to do, and certainly to sustain, than a more conventional relationship where you have dinner and discuss movies. You are going to have to build something between the two of you. Some way to bear your proximity. And that something is love, which very often presents itself as a story. How did you meet? What did you like about each other? What were you doing before you met? How did you overcome the normal barriers of politeness in order to be able to kiss or go to bed with each other? What were the problems in the beginning? How did you resolve them? What kind of artifice did you manage to construct between the two of you in order to tolerate each other's presence? So love itself is a form of storytelling. You could almost say that it's not that there's love and then there's writing about love, but that love itself is already a bit like writing. It's something you make up in relation to another person.

People in love very often simultaneously start writing, either in diaries, or poems or stories, or sending letters or emails or sometimes hundreds of text messages. And when things go wrong, they often write or text about that too. Sometimes, of course, the writing can't contain it, and the person has to supplement the writing by speaking. And when their friends tire of the speaking they go and see a therapist.

Benjamin was a writer who experienced this phenomenon to a really extreme degree. He wrote for a living, as a journalist, and had a rather tempestuous love life. He'd fall in love and the guy would be fantastic, and then six months later he would be a jerk and it would all be over. His journalism was a constant thing – it was a job, and he quite liked it. But it didn't give him any special enjoyment. His romantic poetry was something else. It came accompanied by all sorts of horrible physical effects – dizziness, palpitations, insomnia, sickness. And there would be tons of it – once he started writing he would find it very hard to stop. Once he wrote a hundred poems in a week. The content of his work was pretty consistent – 'What's happening? Why is it happening? Do I want it to happen? How do other people experience it? Why is it happening with this person? What is love? What does it all mean?' An endless series of questions and attempts at answers. He would sometimes get his poetry published, and he saw it as his proper work, with the journalism just there to support him in between outbursts. But something about it was unbearable. The quantity of excitement bound up in it was too much. When it was happening everything else in his life would fall apart. He wouldn't eat, his bills wouldn't get paid and it was hard to do his other work.

As well as writing, Benjamin would want to have conversations all the time, and he'd get confused about which was the thing he *really* wanted to be doing. Was he writing because it was impossible to find enough people who could bear to discuss things with him? Would he alienate all his friends, and his lover, by being so eager to talk? In other words, was writing a kind of poor substitute for a proper human exchange? Or was it what he really wanted to do? He would also want to read about love in these moments: Shakespeare's sonnets, Dennis Cooper, Christopher Isherwood, even the kitsch gay romances of Scott Whittier – anything that promised answers. But this would make him feel even more crazy; there wasn't time for all the things he needed to do. There was no way he could read, write and speak even nearly as much as he wanted to. As Benjamin described it, he really just wanted to engage in an endless dialogue with his lover, to tell him things about himself and ask him questions and know everything he could possibly know about him. But there was an impossibility about it, not only because no one really has the time to do that sort of thing – they have to work, eat and sleep – but also because there was obviously no limit to it, except death. There would always be one more question. And so it would tip over into fantasies about him and his boyfriend killing each other, as if that would be the only adequate way to register a proper love. This idea was very frightening to him – he was a polite and mild-mannered person – so all his efforts were directed towards trying to pull back from that. It was also pretty clear to him that it would be a quick way to lose a boyfriend – to let him know that you seriously thought a lot about bumping him off. So speaking to other friends, or in analysis, or doing his writing presented themselves as the only ways to stave off the violence of his feelings.

In Benjamin's analysis he would talk about what writing meant to him – his parents were both writers, and there'd always been lots of writers around while he was growing up. Writing was the activity that seemed to hold the highest value in his family. Was he writing to please his father, displace his mother, make his brother jealous? He'd also talk about the relationship itself. What kind of fantasy was being activated by the love affair? Who did the guy remind him of? What was he trying to work out with him? The usual kind of therapeutic stuff. It was all interesting enough to him, but it obviously didn't touch the problem he was running up against, which seemed to be this: as soon as he began trying to get satisfaction from someone else in a love relationship, he would find himself confronted with the limits of words and speech. There was something radically senseless about the whole enterprise. There is nothing sensible you can say about love and sex. It doesn't add up. Why try to do this thing with this person? What is the thing and who is the person? Neither question can be satisfactorily answered.

So, for Benjamin, love invariably opened up a really terrifying chasm which threatened to completely engulf him. And the only way to stop himself falling down the hole was to have something to say about the specifics and details of what was going on. None of it would solve the problem, but it would at least put a kind of safely net over the void. In other words, he seemed to be using writing, and speech – although speech was less dependable because it relied on the willingness of other people to listen – to immerse himself in sense-making as such, in order to have *something* to say. And he was doing it as if two lives depended on it, which maybe explains how it became so incredibly pressing. It was a sustained attempt at making sense of a frightening enigma. Benjamin's case seems to show something about the link between love and madness. Love is a delusion, and his writing was a means of trying to deal with a mystery, to give it a face and domesticate it a little in order to be able to bear it.

There has often been a question as to whether fictions about love are 'healthy' or 'unhealthy'. In *Madame Bovary* we see a woman ruin her life over a romantic ideal picked up from cheap novels. But it seems that in Benjamin's case romantic texts were somehow necessary. Not just the production of them, but the reading of other people's. He would say that, in the awful state of being in love (the 'limerent' bit), it didn't matter too much whether you read a camp romcom or Shakespeare. Both appeared to him to be aiming at basically the same thing – at having something, anything, to say about the impossible thing we call love.

Art Appreciation

Of course, words aren't the only things people can use when they get really desperate. Music and pictures can do the job too. Plenty of painters and composers have been driven to fits of crazed production by difficult love affairs. Beethoven is well known for his sentimental attachments to a number of different women – none of whom he married. He seems to have specialized in falling for aristocratic women whose parents didn't entirely approve of him. And this may even have been his unconscious game plan.

He appears to have had the idea that marriage would interfere with his work, but that romance was somehow productive. There is a story, which may or may not be a little bit embellished, concerning his famous bagatelle, *Für Elise* (which translates as 'for Elise'). At the age of forty the composer fell madly in love with the eighteen-year-old Therese Malfatti. He wrote this beautiful, wistful piece of music with her in mind and planned to play it at her father's house on the night he was going to ask her to marry him. Perhaps because the idea of marriage was secretly so horrific to him, he got incredibly drunk, to the point of being unable to play the piano. And also to the point of being unable to propose in front of Therese's father. All he could manage in his inebriated state was to scrawl 'für Therese' at the top of his sheet of music. Evidently his handwriting was quite affected by the alcohol because the piece has been known as *Für Elise* ever since.

There's also the fact that love affairs can sometimes be counter-productive workwise. After things didn't work out between Beethoven and his anonymous 'immortal beloved' he went into a four-year slump, hardly producing anything. Later pieces, like the Ninth Symphony, are no longer informed by romance, but are said to be far more spiritual. As Beethoven wrote in his diary in 1812, 'For thee there is no longer any happiness except in thyself, in thy art.' Love was no longer a spur, but a block and he felt better off without it.

The English poet and painter Dante Gabriel Rossetti repeatedly drew, painted and wrote poems about Elizabeth Siddal as if to contain or pin down whatever it was that he found so exciting about her. His parents thought she was too common for him, so were against marriage, which evidently led to their relationship being excitingly, devastatingly on/off. When he finally married her she was so sick from her laudanum addiction (caused, in part, by her misery over his infidelities) that she had to be carried on the five-minute walk to the church. When she finally died of an overdose after losing their baby, Rossetti buried his poems nestled in her hair – and then had her exhumed a little while later in order to get the poems back. Apparently the hair was still looking good. Not long after she died he resumed relations with his mistress and housekeeper, Fanny Cornforth, whom he found exciting enough to do sixty paintings of, in spite of the fatness which earned her the affectionate nickname 'Elephant'. (I'm sure he meant it well.)

It hardly needs saying that love can make you make stuff. The evidence can be found in every library, cinema, gallery and concert hall in the world. And you don't need to be a specialist to be propelled into action. Plenty of people who've previously had no urge to write, sing or paint suddenly find themselves knocking out poems or songs in the throes of a new romance. Even if their urges don't culminate in artefacts, people in love are very likely to find themselves trying to express their feelings in erotic texts and emotionally charged emails. You might say that the sudden appearance of another important person alerts us to a gap in ourselves. Suddenly we have something to lose. Something important to us is very clearly located outside us, beyond our control. We definitely aren't quite whole. Covering screens, canvases or pieces of paper might be a way to deal with the emergence of this void.

And even if you don't find yourself moved to verse, a very common effect of love is that you suddenly find yourself far more affected by other people's efforts. Like Benjamin, with his renewed appreciation of Shakespeare, you may suddenly understand what Johnny Cash means by a 'Ring of Fire'. And when you screw it all up you can fully appreciate the Sugababes' 'About You Now'. (But *which* of the Sugababes wants to 'bring yesterday back around'? Who does the 'I' in the song refer to? Do they all suffer the same romantic tribulations simultaneously, or is one of them really hurting while the other two merely harmonize in sympathy?) The madness that causes other people to produce songs/artworks/books suddenly speaks to your own madness and even promises to subdue it. If somebody else has felt it, then maybe you aren't that bad after all.

An occasional counterpart to this is that your lover's texts and emails may become totally enigmatic to you. While every song in the universe is addressed to you personally, an email with your name at the top is harder to decode. What are they *really* trying to tell you? Perhaps you show it to your friends in the hope that they will be able to read it better. They say, 'It's all fine. They love you. Shut up.' But what do they know? If a strange sense of meaninglessness can present itself in the face of love, then meaning-making may become very important. The meanings of stories and songs are good because they help to give form to your overwhelming feelings. Perhaps music – especially without lyrics – is exceptionally good because it seems to mean something without being too explicit about what. You can make it mean what you like. In clinical forms of madness – paranoid

psychosis, say, as opposed to mere sentimental loopiness –
meaning becomes a problem. Meanings are attributed to previously meaningless events. One of the first unnerving signs
of insanity is often the sense that the world is sending you
messages. Car number-plates are communicating with you, as
are birds and dogs. But, from the point of view of a supposedly
sane person, it's you that's putting the messages there. You are
compensating for the perplexing indecipherability of the world
around you by filling it up with significance. So you might say
that in love we do the same. We look for meanings everywhere.
And we find them. The most banal lyrics of pop songs suddenly
reveal themselves as being full of import. And your lover's texts
are so brimming with polysemantic complexity they threaten to
make your brain explode. 'C u l8r. x' becomes Joycean in its
textual density; there's no way you can get to the bottom of it. So
the only way to mop up the excess may be to produce something
of your own – a book, a tune or a new word – or to shoot yourself
in the head. And failing that, you could always turn to one of
those tried and tested cures for love – move in together or have
a baby.

4·

When Will I be Loved?

What to do when you aren't loved back

♥ ♥

*In which we pick up tricks from Eric Clapton and
Mills and Boon in the hope that we can learn
how to love and be loved in return*

NOTHING TAKES THE TASTE OUT OF PEANUT BUTTER
LIKE UNREQUITED LOVE.

Charlie Brown

There is a story even shorter than 'Once upon a time there were two people who met and lived happily ever after.' It's also a considerably better story. It concerns a tragic loss but, thankfully, it has a happy ending. And it contains only two words: fort-da. Translated into English, it means 'gone ... there'. Something was missing, and then it reappeared. According to Terry Eagleton in *Literary Theory: An Introduction*, 'even the most complex narratives can be read as variants on this model'. Why bother to read Tolstoy when you can compress the essence of his work into two syllables? ('Fort-da' wouldn't get you through a ten-hour flight, though.) Something disappeared, its absence was awful, and then it came back again. This thing may be a person, a group of people, or even a vague sense of life being okay. Sometimes, as in *The Great Gatsby*, it disappears for a very long time, then comes back, then disappears again almost immediately. Sometimes its coming back causes all sorts of problems, as in *Wuthering Heights*. If you are really unlucky the thing appears just once and then you don't see it again for years and years, as happened in the case of Dante and Beatrice. Stories of unrequited love are fort-da in reverse: 'there … gone'. And this course of events is invariably a source of terrible suffering for the person experiencing it.

Fort-da is the game Freud famously observed his eighteen-month-old grandson playing. Apparently the boy wasn't massively developed for his age (nice vote of confidence, Grandad!). He wasn't speaking much, but he was thought to be admirably mature in that he didn't cry when his mother left him. One of his favourite pastimes was to throw his toys into awkward places and then, with a look of satisfaction, say 'o-o-o-o'. One of the few words he sort of knew how to say was 'o-o-o-o' and everyone in the family agreed it meant 'fort', or 'gone'. One day Freud came across the boy playing with a spool attached to a cotton thread. He was repeatedly throwing it over the side of his cot – where it was concealed by a curtain – and making his customary noise. Then he would pull the string and make the spool reappear, joyfully exclaiming 'da!' ('there!'). From this Freud deduced that he was getting enjoyment from controlling presence and absence. Unlike his mother, who vanished when she vanished and came back when she came back, the spool's appearances and disappearances were within his control.

Of course, his mother's movements might also have been controllable if only he knew how to do it. Crying didn't work every time. In fact he seemed to be congratulated for *not* making a fuss. Letting her go without a tantrum was clearly a good idea if he wanted her to like him; being a 'good boy' was a winner. And she always *did* come back, at least in his experience.

The whole question of how to keep people there, how to make them come back, and what to do while they're missing is very, very important to a child. The solutions you find to the problem of how to manage important people's absences – which will, in turn, be dictated by the responses of the people themselves – will be an important influence on how you go about love later on. There are those whose mothers never left them to cry, but took them everywhere. Then there are others who were left to cry, in the hope that they might become self-reliant. People from each group will presumably have quite different ideas as to what one can expect from a love object. They will develop different strategies for dealing with absence. You may believe you will get what you want as soon as your lip quivers because, in your experience, that's what generally happens. You may never ask for anything because, as you understand it, people don't like to be put upon in that way.

Of course, this is to oversimplify wildly. Your early expectations will obviously be complicated by later experiences. Perhaps you have been totally spoilt and then you get to school and everyone hates you because you think you can bend people to your will by throwing a wobbler. Perhaps, as soon as you get away from your stern and exacting parents, you find that other people are gentler and more generous than expected. Maybe you exploit them mercilessly. Or perhaps you still can't bear to accept their generosity. Human beings are obviously far too complex to be put into simplistic categories like, 'left to cry in cot = stiff upper lip'. However, your early experiences of the presences and absences of loved ones – and how these are given meaning and managed – are certain to leave their mark.

Unrequited love is an experience of an unbearable absence. It doesn't matter if the person works at the opposite desk and is in your line of vision seven hours a day. What matters is that they don't respond in the way you wish they would. If you somehow let them know that you need or want them, they are utterly unmoved. Perhaps they are even disgusted by your advances. Part of the madness of unrequited love involves imagining what the loved one wants – and then either berating oneself for not possessing the qualities they desire, or trying desperately to attain them. There are pros and cons of either option. The first can lead to insanity, depression and possibly suicide. But on the other hand it also makes it unlikely that you will ever get together with the person and find out how difficult they really are. The second may cause you to make all sorts of improvements to yourself and your circumstances, which may be good, but there's no guarantee it will work. And even if it does, then there's always the worry that the person is simply in love with your money/muscles/silicone breasts, and not with the 'real you'.

To put it unromantically, the problem of unrequited love is, at some level, a problem of *strategy*, so it may be worth looking at a few different cases in order to assess the different ways of handling your unreturned affections.

O-o-o-o! Misery! Misery!

The Latin poet Catullus and the rock star Eric Clapton have a lot in common. Both are uncompromisingly autobiographical, and both suffered intense bouts of unrequited love.

Catullus lived in Italy during the first century BC. He knew lots of important people, many of whom he insulted in his poetry. (To his friend Flavius: 'It's no good keeping quiet about it / You'd not present such fucked-out flanks / If you weren't up to something foolish.') Catullus wrote a number of love poems addressed to a woman called Lesbia. Historians have come to the conclusion that his real-life love was a woman called Clodia, who may have been any one of three sisters of the same name. The prime suspect is the sister who was the wife of the Roman praetor, Metellus Celer. This Clodia was the only one who was married – as Lesbia is – and was clearly a bit of a rotten apple, having shamelessly cheated on her husband and possibly poisoned him.

In the poems, Lesbia goes from being hopelessly idealized to viciously denigrated. While she starts off as the best thing ever, ever, ever, she ends up as a heartless trollop. It appears that Lesbia/Clodia and the poet did actually have a full-blown affair at some point, but it didn't work out. The poems addressed to her are about as painful as poetry can be. In this one she's sitting opposite another man, laughing, leaving Catullus feeling totally destroyed:

> … no sooner, Lesbia,
> Do I look at you than there's no power left me
> Of speech in my mouth
>
> But my tongue's paralysed, invisible flame
> Courses down through my limbs, with din of their own
> My ears are ringing and twin darkness covers
> The light of my eyes.

In another poem he imagines giving her three thousand three hundred kisses. And elsewhere, when he describes the death of her pet sparrow, he can hardly get over the grief. It's not known how long Catullus' impossible love went on for (he refers to it as a 'long love' in Poem 76), but it's been estimated at about five years. For a man who lived to the age of thirty, that's quite a large portion of his life. When he finally gives up on Lesbia he seems to be pretty furious – she's just a faithless floozie who doesn't give a damn about him. But if she hadn't been so romantically inconsistent, he might not have created his life's work. Catullus, like Benjamin in the previous chapter, seems to have used his writing to process unbearable feelings. (Though, if we take Freud seriously, these may have been unbearable feelings that gave him a certain amount of perverse enjoyment.)

♥

Eric Clapton suffered the misfortune of falling for his best friend's wife. Pattie Boyd was married to George Harrison when Clapton met and fell in love with her. Clapton and Harrison were working together at the time, and Clapton would often go and hang out at his married friends' house. He had the sense that Pattie wasn't too happy with George, although he wasn't sure what to do about it. Initially, doing nothing seemed like the most appropriate option. So Clapton did nothing and went completely loopy. At the time a friend of his was in the process of converting to Islam. This friend introduced Clapton to the ancient Arabic story of Layla and Majnun (which translates as *Layla and the Madman*). In the story – which is apparently based on real events – the poet and shepherd, Qays ibn al-Mulawwah, falls madly in love with a girl called Layla, but is prevented from marrying her by her father. Shortly after blocking their wedding, Layla's dad marries her off to someone else. Before this, Qays ibn al-Mulawwah was writing ordinarily mad love poetry to Layla. But after her wedding he goes completely off his tree, runs off into the wilderness and starts ranting in verse and writing poems in the sand with a stick. His family were understandably worried and would leave food out for him. This way, he managed to survive for quite some time. But when Layla left town with her husband, then became ill and died, he couldn't bear it any more and dropped dead himself – but not before chiselling a final three verses onto a rock.

While Qays ibn al-Mulawwah lived in the seventh century, his story continued to be told in Persian, Turkish and Latin, and may even have been an influence on Shakespeare's *Romeo and Juliet* (although there's a fair amount of academic quibbling about this). Anyhow, its effect on Eric Clapton was to cause him to identify completely with the poet and to write his famous song 'Layla', which is all about being grovellingly in love. According to the music journalist Dave Marsh, 'there are few moments in the repertoire of recorded rock where a singer or writer has reached so deeply into himself that the effect of hearing them is akin to witnessing a murder, or a suicide … [T]o me, *Layla* is the greatest of them.' It certainly seemed to work on Pattie. When Clapton lured her to a flat in South Kensington in order to play her the song she found it 'the most moving song [she] had ever heard'. Unfortunately, her husband managed to track her down and, in spite of Clapton's forthright announcement that he was in love with Pattie, she still went home with Harrison. At some point in the shenanigans, Clapton turned up drunk at the Harrisons' house for a 'guitar duel'. As Pattie recalled in her autobiography, 'George handed him a guitar and an amp – as an 18th-century gentleman might have handed his rival a sword'. Clapton and Harrison played late into the night, sending sallies of riffs and solos back and forth. Although it wasn't formally announced, Clapton came out the winner (unsurprisingly). Harrison's playing had apparently become a little hysterical in places, while Clapton had kept his musical cool.

The good news is that Clapton did eventually get the girl, and that it all worked out so amicably that George Harrison even came to their wedding. The bad news is that Eric Clapton turned out to be an equally crappy husband, banning Pattie from joining him on tour and occasionally impregnating other women. They split up a decade or so later. Still, he wrote lots more songs about her. (Most famously, *Wonderful Tonight*, while he was annoyed with her for taking so long to get ready for a party.) And then she wrote a rather charming autobiography to recover from her two gruelling marriages. In terms of the mind-baby head count, the match was an overall success.

Great Heights and Crushing Lows

Catullus shows us that an unrequited love may even include a sexual relationship – the defining feature is that the person doesn't return your feelings with the same intensity. Clapton is a good example of someone who managed to turn unrequited love around – using the very product of the pain itself (the song) – although he then had to deal with the unromantic aftermath otherwise known as marriage.

So what other strategies have people employed? In *The Great Gatsby* and *Wuthering Heights* we see a similar tactic adopted by both unrequited lovers, but it turns out not to be a recipe for happiness. In each case the heroes, Jay Gatsby and Heathcliff, are deemed too poor to marry the women they desire. Both Daisy Buchanan and Cathy Earnshaw are a little bit grabby and choose wealth over passion, though they soon find that the houses and dresses aren't as fulfilling as they hoped they'd be (plus Daisy is wealthy in her own right and could have afforded them anyway). But while Daisy and Cathy have been getting on with their less-than-fulfilling family lives, their first loves have been out making their way in the world. When Gatsby and Heathcliff reappear, it's with a definite air of: 'You picked *that* loser. If only you had more patience you could have married *me*.' The sudden re-emergence of the sexy guys, now with wads of cash in the bank, causes a few ripples in each of the ladies' marriages. Daisy succumbs to an affair, with fatal consequences. Cathy doesn't, but dies in childbirth saying, 'You and Edgar have broken my heart, Heathcliff! And you both come to bewail the deed to me, as if you were the people to be pitied.'

Of course, at the time both books were written, women's lots were enormously different from whatever they are today. (For more on this, see chapter seven.) Marriage was pretty much the only means women had to make their way in the world, so you can't get too snotty with these female characters for the messes they got themselves into. (Or at least not with Cathy – Daisy *is* a bit of a silly bitch.) For now, the point is that Gatsby and Heathcliff both went off and did whatever they had to do in order to make themselves loveable. In terms of the fort-da schema, they worked out how to bring the object back. They couldn't be loved because they were not men of means. So they became men of means and, lo and behold, they found their love returned. There are lots of ways of understanding this. You might say it was all very Darwinian. Daisy and Cathy were the prettiest girls around, so it stood to reason that they had to bag the most powerful, presentable men on the block. The husbands they chose, Tom Buchanan and Edgar Linton, could give them all the food and shelter they wanted, as well as providing handsomely for their offspring. Although there seems to be an element of affection involved for both women, their marriages are guided primarily by economic factors. The loves these women feel for Gatsby and Heathcliff are impossible loves, initially for monetary/Darwinian reasons and then because the women are married. But the impossibility of these loves is also what gives them their appearance of authenticity. While Daisy and Cathy are making the best of it with Tom and Edgar, they *can't help* loving Gatsby and Heathcliff. (In Schopenhauerian terms, the will of the species might be better served by the disallowed pairings – Cathy and Heathcliff's children would surely have been *gorgeous*.) However, Gatsby and Heathcliff can't simply say, 'Oh well, she loves me, but society's stacked against us so what can she do?' Both men are devastated by what they see as rejections. They make sure they do everything within their means to persuade these women of their worthiness, even if it's obviously going to bring about disaster.

As we said at the beginning of the chapter, the problem for the unrequited lover is how to make himself loveable to the other person. And this problem goes to the heart of what a human being is. While other animals can rely on luscious tail feathers – or just put up with a lesser mate if their feathers leave something to be desired – human beings put a lot of thought into making themselves loveable. While it can't be denied that there are standards of human beauty that people in any given culture seem loosely to agree on, it's also true that a GSOH (Good Sense of Humour) or OHAC (Own House and Car) can get you quite a long way.

The problem of how to make oneself loveable has tradition-ally been different for men compared with women. In the olden days men could provide goods, and women could be pretty and/or motherly. Of course it's always been more blurry than that. Women have long appreciated a strong jaw and lean physique, while men haven't exactly been unmoved by large dowries. And again, values vary within different societies and during different periods, and from family to family – and even between one sibling and another within the same family. Perhaps one brother can be loved for his studiousness, while the other – sensing the hopelessness of academic competition – angles for affection with his mischievous sense of humour. Making oneself loveable is a huge and perplexing issue. One of the signs of Dorothy Tennov's 'limerence' was a tendency to go out and buy new clothes, and as one of the symptoms of an uncomfortable liking for someone, this seems to be spot on. Buying new clothes may be an attempt to shoehorn oneself into an image you imagine the other person will like. Maybe you try to look more like them. Or maybe you try to look like their ex. Or maybe you have your own bizarre notion of the type of person someone like them would desire. In any case, you do what you can to try to make yourself an appealing prospect, whether it's getting a haircut, polishing your shoes, or paying more attention than usual to your level of grooming. This is a more sophisticated form of fluffing up your feathers.

Cheap Advice

So far in this chapter we have looked at writers and artists who people largely agree are quite good. That's all very well from a cultural point of view, but the notoriously unhappy endings suggest that these people are pretty bad at offering placatory counsel or encouraging models. If you look to Catullus for advice about unrequited love, all you're going to get is that it's really a grim lot and that the person you love is probably a total bitch or bastard anyway. Eric Clapton's example is more cheering in that he manages to do what most unrequited lovers would like to do; he uses his skill to turn his mopeyness into a valuable artefact that causes the desired object to fall in love with him – a more sophisticated and dignified version of Dido's tears (not to mention more effective). But *still* he ends up unhappy. Qays ibn al-Mulawwah is barely worth mentioning; going mad and writing in the sand with a stick is a non-starter. Gatsby and Heathcliff offer yet more unfortunate examples, both in that they do the obvious and go off and get rich, *and* in that it all blows up in their faces.

Dealing with unrequited love is a strategic issue, but none of these strategies seem that impressive (although I have to announce Clapton the winner, despite preferring all the other works to 'Layla' by a mile). If you want tips on how to be a good writer you should certainly look at Catullus or Brontë, but if you need proper romantic advice you might actually be better off reading a Mills and Boon. You may not enjoy it, but if you can stomach the prose style you may be forced to recognize the fact that it offers far more serviceable guidelines than anything on a university reading list.

Susan Mallery's offering, *Falling for Gracie*, is an excellent blueprint for frustrated lovers. While it may contain sentences like, 'Her heart rate increased to a beat per second far more normal for a hummingbird than a twenty-eight-year-old woman who knew better', it also has plenty to say on the theme of upping one's loveability. At the beginning of the story Gracie, our heroine, is already a legend. At the age of fourteen she fell in love with a boy called Riley Whitefield, and the whole town knew about it. Apparently she wasn't much of a looker and Riley duly ignored her, opting instead for some leggy cheerleader type called Pam. Gracie took the rejection badly and launched into a Majnun-style display of craziness. She locked a skunk in his car in order to ruin his hot date with Pam, and threw herself at his wheels in a futile attempt at preventing his wedding. The local paper got hold of the story, and thus were born the infamous 'Gracie Chronicles'. While some of the old ladies found it rather sweet, Gracie became the brunt of malicious gossip to the extent that her mother sent her away to live with an aunt and uncle in LA. So, the backstory is one of unrequited love. And also of extremely bad tactics. Putting skunks in people's cars is no way to make them love you. It's a way to alienate them and make them think you're pathetic and possibly dangerous.

We join Gracie back in Los Lobos, whence she has returned for the first time in fourteen years. Her younger sister is getting married and Gracie's there to bake the cake. Every granny in town is out to remind her of her insane crush on Riley. As are her spiteful mother and two heinous sisters. But Gracie's over it now. She's a grown-up celebrity baker – and good-looking to boot. She doesn't do silly crushes any more.

Unfortunately Riley is back in town too – and divorced! He's hoping to get over his bad-boy reputation and is running for mayor. In an extremely ludicrous bit of plotting, Gracie's sister finds some implausible reason to send Gracie round to his house to take photos through his windows. The flash goes off, Gracie is caught, and she and Riley come face to face. Riley, of course, is dark, dangerous and denim-clad. And he has a very stupid-sounding earring. Gracie tells herself that she doesn't feel a thing. But as the two meet again and again in the shoebox-town that is Los Lobos, Riley can't help noticing that Gracie is rather nice these days. Not only does she have big boobs and glossy hair, she is also funny, self-deprecating and extremely kind. She always seems to be going out of her way for other people, and she never gets sick of offering Riley slices of cake. Sparks fly. Really, that's how they put it.

Needless to say lots of poxy things happen, including pages and pages of nauseating sex between the two main characters. And not even just towards the end. You have been warned – *I* didn't know it was coming: 'At the same moment he claimed her mouth, he pushed deep into her, replacing his fingers with something far larger and more impressive.' It's so horrible to know this about Gracie and Riley. They are Barbies, not rutting beasts. When did Mills and Boon novels get like that? But the most important thing is that Gracie finds a way to go from psycho-skunk-bitch to temptress. So how did she do it? First of all, she underwent a series of extremely unfortunate experiences, beginning with her father's death when she was thirteen. Gracie was apparently his favourite, so the loss was particularly devastating; she was suddenly stuck in a house with three other females who'd probably all envied and hated her for years. The classic Cinderella set-up.

As the story explains it, she immediately turned her attention to Riley, the slightly older boy next door. Perhaps the grief had made her lose her sense of propriety, or perhaps being her father's favourite had given her false ideas about her charms. Anyhow, she proceeded to persecute him with her affection. Or to 'love him with all her heart', as the local paper chose to represent it. This notoriety compounded Gracie's problems. It made her feel special (as she had done while her father was alive) but it also made the women in her family despise her even more. Without her father's protection, they were able to give free rein to their aggression, so they palmed her off on a childless aunt and uncle. On the bright side, these relatives turned out to be quite nice. On the grim side, they were killed in a car crash. So Gracie had to find her way in the world without special protection. She wasn't exceptional for *anyone* any more. She was just a piece of human flotsam. She had to work out what other people wanted from her, in order to survive. Contrary to what her sisters (and Pam-the-cheerleader) believe, they don't want vain, uppity tarts who are only after your money. It actually turns out that other people want pleasant, honest, unassuming women, who also know how to make really fancy cakes. In other words, Gracie had to give up a large chunk of her narcissism and join the struggling masses. She had to stop thinking she was innately important or extraordinary and get on with developing some exchangeable skills. There is a side of this that's rather depressing; Gracie had to become a 'nice girl' in order to be loved by a 'bad boy'. Thanks for cowing women in the name of entertainment yet again, Mills and Boon! But there is also a side of it that's very astute.

A large number of people these days believe that Freud's Oedipus complex is defunct. Apparently it was 'disproven', or simply found unnecessary sometime in the last century. Or maybe it was just too distasteful even to think about. Even in the 1940s and 1950s, when people still gave it some credit, they often had the idea that you either had a complex or you didn't — and that having one wasn't very good. It meant you were still in love with one of your parents and were therefore no use to anyone else. But the Oedipus complex isn't really like that. It's more a way of explaining how human beings are socialized. And a large part of socialization involves learning to deal with disappointment. In Freud's schema we are all submitted to a set of disillusionments and frustrations. We have to concede that we are not at the centre of our mother's universe. We learn to give way to other siblings, our father, our mother's boyfriend, her work. (Needless to say, Freud himself didn't name these last two competitors.) We also have to give up on the idea of simply doing or getting what we want and learn to conform to a set of rules. And this is where Jacques Lacan stretches the Oedipus complex to a point where it almost doesn't look like Freud's any more. This set of laws may be laid down by the biological father — as in the old school Oedipal decree, 'You can't have your mother to yourself, she's mine too.' Or it may come from elsewhere — the child's school, a stepfather, an aunt or an uncle. In Lacanian jargon one might say, 'Stop trying to be the phallus for the mother!' (Strangely, this phrase hasn't caught on in most families, yet.) In ordinary speech it may go something more like, 'Get over your mum and learn to get along with other people.' And, as with the 'father' – who may actually be any number of agencies – for 'mother' read 'primary carer'. You have to stop trying to be *everything* for your primary carer and get on with being *something* for the rest of the world. Lacan calls the place from which this intervention comes the Name-of-the-Father, meaning anything that forces the child to give up pole position in its own mind and submit to the rules of its family, and of its culture.

Lacan's argument goes that, in the olden days, the threat used in order to bring a child into line could be boiled down to, 'Do as I say or I'll chop your penis off – unless you are a girl, in which case it's basically happened already, you poor thing.' Some unfortunate children may actually have had this sort of thing said to them. Others didn't need to hear it said aloud because they were already so worried by the thought that it inevitably arrived as the hidden subtext of any telling-off. Jacques Lacan's reinterpretation of the Oedipus complex tries to solve the problem of what goes on with girls – they have nothing to chop off, so what happens to them instead? Why would they bother to socialize themselves? His idea is that there is an Oedipal threat just as terrifying as physical castration, if not more so. And that it can be used equally effectively on boys and girls: the threat of the loss of love. Children know that a life without love would be gruesome. For children, love is a matter of survival; your loveability is what ensures your continued existence. If you are unloveable you may find yourself left on a mountainside to die. So when your carers find fault with you, it's a matter of some seriousness. While it may be annoying to be separated from your mother, told not to masturbate (i.e. separated from *yourself*) and generally coerced into doing the sorts of helpful, unselfish things that go against your every inclination, you do it (or at least a bit of it) because if you don't, they might not love you any more. In a sense, you accept what seems like a decrease in love in the hope that this will ensure the continuation of love – albeit in a lesser form.

The upside of the Oedipus complex is that it relieves you of the anxiety of trying to please someone absolutely. The bad news is that it tells you that this is something that can't be done. You are not good enough or interesting enough or potent enough to be everything for anyone. You are just another lacking being, full of faults, shortcomings and weaknesses.

On realizing this, you have a number of choices. You can spend your whole life trying to prove to the world that you are, in fact, perfect – that you've been misjudged. This is the Gatsby/ Heathcliff position. Or you can say, 'Yes, I'm really crap, aren't I?' and set out to demonstrate just how useless you are, which is what Young Werther did. Alternatively, you can say, 'I may be a bit dodgy, but I'm going to do my best and see how far it gets me.' This is basically Gracie's position and, of the three, it could be said to be the most 'healthy' (i.e. the most useful to society).

But Gracie had to learn this the hard way. Initially she was petulant and assumed that she simply deserved to be loved. We might say – at the risk of offending the right-thinking people who believe it's wrong to psychoanalyse literary figures – that

Gracie has undergone a second round of Oedipal battering. (On second thoughts, I believe Mills and Boon characters are exempt from the ban.) From the little we know of Gracie's backstory we might assume that she emerged from the first round, aged five or so, a little bit too full of herself. Instead of making an incisive cut and severing Gracie from her infantile dreams of ultimate loveability, Gracie's father has effectively said, 'I love you and think you're the most special girl in this family.' Gracie has formed the impression that she can stop being the phallus for her mother in order to get on with being some sort of dolly for her father. She hasn't *really* had to give anything up. While she has the preferential love of her father she doesn't need to get along too well with the other women in her family, or to work out how to make herself appealing to the boys at her school. In other words, she is utterly unbearable. So when Gracie loses her father, is ejected by her immediate family, then loses her aunt and uncle she is, in effect, resubmitted to the Oedipal trauma and has to do the work she failed to do the first time around. She has to become humble, without being self-pitying, and to work out what she has to give that people actually want.

Throughout the story the grown-up Gracie impresses Riley with her superbly well-socialized character. No longer is she a machine-like romantic maniac. Now she has doubts, but they don't completely crush her. She concedes when she's wrong, and sticks to her opinion when she thinks she may be right. She lets go of the things she wants in the name of the greater good. When she thinks she may be pregnant (they didn't use a condom the first time, the idiots) she doesn't try to use it to bag her man.

She tells the truth, even when it makes her look bad. And when Riley threatens to blow the mayoral election simply in order to prove that he really, truly loves her, she refuses to let him do it. Gracie has become a lovely, realistic, disappointed optimist. And in this state she is fit to be loved. (Plus the hair and boobs.)

The only trace of Gracie's terrible concession to normality is her dodgy stomach. Being so nice all the time is making her sick. At the first sign of emotional trouble she reaches for her ever-handy pack of Setlers Tums. Initially it seems like an odd character trait in a romantic heroine – she's always referring to her lurching acid and cramps, even popping the pills in front of Riley on a regular basis. But if that's the cost of giving up her all-consuming egotism, it's worth it. Gracie gets her man.

Lessons in Love

If the name of the game is somehow to bring the object back into your orbit, then the best way to do it may be to show that you can live without it. When Catullus sees Lesbia with another man and goes completely bonkers, it's easy to understand why Lesbia might find this a bit trying. While lots of people may imagine they'd like to be loved absolutely, if anyone ever attempts to do this to you, you soon discover that it's a pain in the butt. Suddenly you have no freedom and everything upsets them. It's a bit like being a new parent – only grown-up babies aren't nearly so endearing. Heathcliff, too, seems to expect rather a lot from Cathy; that she give up any interest in worldly possessions and commit herself only to their love. While poor old Edgar gets a bad press for being a bit weedy and boring, I'm not sure marriage to Heathcliff would have been a bundle of laughs either. What would they do together after the first fortnight in bed? And, as for Gatsby, his love for Daisy is plainly creepy and weird. When Nick Carraway, the narrator, says to him, 'You can't repeat the past,' Gatsby immediately comes back with, 'Can't repeat the past?… Why of course you can!' Is he really referring to a cool night in his and Daisy's youth when the sidewalk was white with moonlight, etc.? Or is he talking about a much, much older, more infantile kind of love, in which the person he loves would dote on him exclusively?

While falling in love may inevitably stir up echoes of our earliest relations, this needn't mean we are reduced to blubbering brats. With luck, between then and now we have been through the mill a bit, had strips torn off us, occasionally been kicked in the teeth. If our loved one leaves the room, we trust them to come back. And if they don't, so be it. We've been through worse. We don't need to keep them on a piece of string – they can disappear down the back of a piece of furniture (or even across an ocean) and we won't keep tugging at their leash.

Right from the beginning, Gracie is at pains to show Riley that she is over him, that she really doesn't need him any more. She doesn't do this by being nasty or petulant – she's always extremely courteous. Nastiness would be a sure sign that she was still hung up. By being civil she sends him the message that she's fully recovered. When the affair begins and they have their pregnancy scare, she further proves her independence by calmly letting him know he's free to leave. This way Riley receives the idea that marrying Gracie wouldn't be like voluntarily walking into a very cramped cage. She might even let him carry on spending time on his precious oil rigs. (All those men cooped up together watching the fashion channel! You can see why he misses it.)

When you love someone who doesn't love you back then, really, that's just your tough luck. You can hate them, or yourself, but unless you can turn it into poetry (or duel-winning guitar riffs) there isn't much point in getting worked up about it. Remember, no one is ever going to love you in the way your mother failed to. (And if she succeeded I pity you more.) If they appear to, it's because they are mad. And, if you're loving someone from afar, you probably don't really love *them* anyhow, you're just in love with an idea.

However, if you insist on believing in your own fictions and you're determined to get the other person to believe in them too, then according to our brief foray into comparative literature, the cardinal rules for unrequited lovers are:

* Spend time away from them. Maybe even getting rich.
* But don't try to bring them round with money – it's not nice.
* Be gracious and offer cake.
* Don't grizzle when they're nice to other people.
* Do write a song or poem about them. But only show it to them if you have proven artistic talents.
* However, no sand poems.

* Do let them see that you are a proper grown-up who has suffered, and knows how to let things go.
* Don't expect them to give up everything to be with you (however good you look on horseback).
* If you must host big parties in their neighbourhood, make sure you enjoy the parties yourself.
* Don't try to show them that you're perfect. You're as lame as everyone else.
* And, if you seriously want them to love you, *try* not to put a skunk in their car.

5.

Marry Me a Little

How to be dedicated without being dull

♥   ♥

*In which we contemplate long-term commitment
and frighten ourselves with Victorian novels, before
finding some solace in* Sex and the City

TAKE IT FROM ME, MARRIAGE ISN'T A WORD, IT'S
A SENTENCE.

King Vidor

In the event that you actually manage to persuade someone to love you, congratulations. Next you will have to deal with the consequences of your choice. Will their work take them to Africa? Will they drink all your savings and beat you up? Or will they become a top lawyer and buy you a five-storey house in Chelsea? And what happens if you suddenly meet someone you like better? It's often said that love is destiny – if you finally find someone and stick with them it will have enormous consequences for the shape and direction of your life. Some things may become possible (children and a joint mortgage), others more difficult (a romantic trip to Hawaii with your child's attractive violin teacher).

In contemporary society, where there is a free-floating notion that you should simply love who you love and not worry about the rest of it, it can come as quite a shock that one's romantic choices continue to carry pragmatic consequences. It can feel almost dirty to admit that your partner's extreme poverty, say, has knock-on effects for you. Surely it shouldn't matter that they can't afford a cup of tea, it's what's in their heart/mind/soul/ pants that counts – as well as their capacity to get on with your friends, go to parties with you, and encourage you to carry on doing the things that really excite you. Almost any reason for choosing someone is thought better than, 'Because s/he seemed like a good financial bet.' But is it? Really? In terms of building a shared existence, perhaps someone's ability to pay the odd bill isn't a totally negligible consideration.

Naturally there are still plenty of people who marry for money, or for a name, but this is largely frowned on. The norm these days is supposedly to get together for the sake of pure, unconditional liking. Having said that, it's important to bear in mind what we learnt from the anthropologists; just because a society upholds a certain ideal, it doesn't necessarily follow that individuals adhere to it. Perhaps this partially explains the low-level fascination with WAGs and other forms of C-list gold-digger; they are going against the sentimental diktats of their culture, so it's always interesting to see how they fare.

Love, Marriages, Horses and Carriages

Given the supposed state of modern society's romantic standards, it's curious that writers like Jane Austen and George Eliot continue to be so popular. Why should we give a damn whether Miss So and So marries a politician or a country curate? Surely all that matters is whether she likes the guy or not. Of course Austen and Eliot are both very concerned with liking and not liking, and their heroines' choices can hardly be reduced to economics. Austen's books have been said to be like very refined zoological studies. The characters have to mate and, like monkeys, they are looking for a combination of animal lust, good breeding and plenty of bananas (and all to be achieved before the end of the season). In other words, there generally has to be a bit of excitement in order for the carriages and mansions to look appealing. A dull or mean person with bags of dough won't do – a good match has to be kind and exciting as well as solvent.

In *Sense and Sensibility* two opposing methods of spouse-choosing are played off against one another. On the one hand there is Marianne, who reads Shakespeare's sonnets (aloud, with lots of expression) and expects to marry only after falling madly in love. On the other hand, there is her older sister, Elinor, who imagines it's wiser to pick a mate along more phlegmatic lines. The book was published in 1811, at a time when passion versus reason was a hot philosophical debate (as it still should be today, because it's not as if we've managed to reach a resolution). Jane Austen ingeniously makes fun of the polar opposition by making Elinor marry for love after a painful, dramatic courtship, while the fruitier Marianne weds a slightly dreary but dependable older man. Basically, you can't know which kind of choice will produce better results – and you may find yourself choosing for reasons that seem quite out of character. In other words, love matches operate according to their own laws, and we just have to bear it and see what happens.

So much has been written about this novel that it's almost painful to join in the cacophony. Is there anything new to be said about it? The solution I found was to watch the movie version, starring Emma Thompson and Kate Winslet, with my seven-year-old daughter, and to see what she made of it. It wasn't an in-depth analysis but at least it was fresh. Her main concern was with what 'old Wallaby' was up to. It's very nice to think of Willoughby as a silly-looking, bouncy animal, because that's what he is, the bounder. She also thought Colonel Brandon was evil. Every time he spoke she said, 'He's lying now, isn't he?' At the end, she looked absolutely horrified and asked, 'But why is Marianne marrying Professor Snape?'

To sum up, you could say that *Sense and Sensibility* is a tale about love, sex and death, or that it's a delightful elaboration of the nature versus culture debate. This would of course be true, but from a certain perspective it's also very clearly a story about why a very pretty but otherwise ordinary girl would switch her affections from a wallaby to a wizard.

George Eliot's books are different from Jane Austen's in that she doesn't merely show us how people get together, but also what happens to them after they've made their choices. In *Daniel Deronda* we see the terrible trouble Gwendolen Harleth gets herself into when she marries the rich and horrible Henleigh Grandcourt (which she does largely in order to avoid getting a job). In *Middlemarch*, too, peculiar marital choices abound.

Virginia Woolf called it 'one of the few English novels written for grown-up people'. It's so full of disappointment, disillusionment and horror at having plumped for the wrong option it's amazing that anyone can actually bear to read it. There's Tertius Lydgate and Rosamond Vincy who have married for completely stupid reasons (she thinks he's posh, he thinks she's pretty) and who find themselves utterly miserable as soon as the illusion cracks. There's poor old Mrs Bulstrode whose loyalty to her dodgy husband forces her into exile with him. And then there's Dorothea Brooke's unfortunate selection of Reverend Edward Casaubon, who looks like a worthy scholar but turns out to be a spiteful, arrogant loser. (Marrying someone who thinks they are the world's best writer, but who doesn't actually do much writing, is a very bad idea. Writers are horrible at the best of times – they are amoral and can't keep secrets – but would-be literary geniuses are the lowest of the low.)

Dorothea is a character you can really root for – she's friendly and clever and cares for the poor. The book begins with the question of how, or even whether, as a woman she can actually do anything interesting and useful with her life. She could marry the rich guy down the road (who's in love with her) and build lots of houses for the less fortunate residents of the village. But she shocks everyone by opting instead for a dried-out old stick of a reverend, and soon discovers that he's not interested in her ideas about mythology, nor is he even all that interested in his own. The Great Work they were going to make together is a dead loss. The only good thing about Dorothea's awful husband is that he drops dead and leaves her all his money well before the end of the book. Now she can get on with plan A: doing good deeds. The only downside is that Revd Casaubon has put a clause in his will forbidding Dorothea to marry his cousin, the dashing, artistic Will Ladislaw. Dorothea is supposedly quite unaware of how much she secretly wants to do just that and dithers around for ages feeling lost and screwed up. Finally, amid thunder and lightning flashes – because even George Eliot wasn't above that sort of meteorological silliness – Dorothea and Will finally admit how much they love each other. Dorothea says they can live without Casaubon's dirty money and they immediately rush off and have kids.

We hear in the postscript that Will does a bit of journalism and local politicking and that Dorothea makes a very nice wife. This would usually qualify as a pretty conclusive happy ending, only Eliot makes it far less simple. Dorothea, by opting to marry a man she actually likes and fancies, makes it impossible for herself to achieve the great things she had hoped for. Without her widow's wad she has had to give up on the building projects and just get on with being nice to the people in her immediate circle. But, as Eliot tells us, 'the growing good of the world is partly dependent on unhistoric acts'; i.e. we shouldn't feel too sad that such an extraordinary woman has given up her great schemes in order to get on with breeding. You can improve the world in small ways as well as in big ones. Be nice to your spouse, your children, your neighbours. In the universal scheme it's not *so* different to designing a cathedral or painting the *Mona Lisa*. It's still quite frustrating to read, though.

The book offers no comfort or advice on romantic decision-making. You can be lucky or unlucky, or anything in between. Its only likeness to a Mills and Boon is in its use of emotionally significant weather. If you make a terrible choice you may be fortunate enough to have a second crack, but that doesn't mean you won't blow it again the next time. Not that Dorothea exactly blew it with Will Ladislaw – it's possibly much nicer to be a reasonably happy wife than a reasonably unhappy but very philanthropic widow – but she certainly gave something up in order to be with him.

Making choices necessarily involves sacrifice. And these sorts of sacrifice are only necessary because we are mortal. If we lived for ever we would be able to try everything out. Because life is finite it can appear to matter greatly whether or not we pick the right stuff. Our love choices are particularly loaded because they involve linking our own will and wishes to those of someone else. For women this has traditionally been far more pressing than it has for men, not only because marriage was sometimes their only means of ensuring a living for themselves, but also because their fertility period is so much shorter. As the first reason has diminished slightly in importance (although a double income is still vital to people who want to live in big houses), this second matter seems to have become even more frighteningly significant. Although we can now supposedly have as much sex as we like with whomever we like, we can't so easily leave pregnancy to chance. We have quite reliable contraceptives, so desperately fancying someone and breeding with them need no longer be linked at all. Accidental pregnancies are far harder to arrange these days. If we are to have a baby we may have to actually *want* it – and this can be far more problematic than having one foisted upon us. Our choice of whether, when and with whom to have a child is bound to be fraught with meaning. Should we wait until our career is established? But is a career ever *really* established? Once it is so-called established, is it really wise to mess it up by taking six months off? Should we have children while we're still at university – where they have cheap crèche facilities – and start working seriously once they have started school? Should we import a five-year-old from China, saving it from an orphanage and ourselves from years of nappy-changing? Should we lie about taking the pill to a one-night stand? Or should we wait for someone we want to spend our lives with, at the risk of missing the boat? Or should we just jump off a cliff because it's all totally meaningless anyway?

These sorts of choices have become agonisingly over-defined. Magazines are full of them, and while the analysis may sometimes seem tediously predictable, these dilemmas have been at the heart of our culture from the very beginning: without them, books, films, songs and television would never have needed to exist. There'd be no stories by the bonfire. No epic poems. And the force that gives these decisions the power to captivate and upset us is death. Death is the vanishing point that organizes any story, whether it features as part of the narrative or not. Marianne Dashwood's marsupial-to-supernatural leap can only be charged with sentimental import due to her inevitable demise. Dorothea Brooke has only one short existence to gamble with and she chooses love and domesticity over grand schemes. You could say that Eliot is the queen of romantic realists in that she makes it clear that people generally have to give something up in order to make love possible. Unlike Austen, who lets the nasty people lose out while the nice people manage to resolve everything, Eliot shows that disappointment and loss may form part of living happily ever after. Doing the thing that best suits you still means giving up a number of other things that might also suit you very well.

In the 1970s and 1980s, when the nuclear threat was at its most imaginarily oppressive, people regularly used to ask each other what they would do with their last four and a half minutes in the event of a nuclear warning. Would you have sex with the first person you could lay your hands on? Eat? Pray? Wank? Kill somebody? Or just sit there, thinking what the hell? Well, in a sense the whole of life is just such a conundrum. Eighty or so years may sound a lot more than four and a half minutes, but you are presented with precisely the same problem: what do you do with your limited time? What would *really* satisfy you? What would you allow yourself to want if you weren't just trying to fit in with other people? Of course the eighty extra years complicate things a little. This is why we have law. If what you most enjoy is killing people then you may find yourself spending a large number of those years in jail. Or you may not get caught. Maybe you think it's worth the risk. Any big decision you make concerning your overall satisfaction (and the only thing that makes a decision big is its relation to satisfaction and enjoyment) is necessarily made in relation to death. Decision-making is morbid. Choosing a partner is one of the gloomiest things you can ever do in that it inevitably – if unconsciously – puts you in contact with the pressing matter of your own annihilation.

Although we've said that women are particularly beholden to the problem of time and mortality where long-term mating is concerned, men are far from exempt. If the problem for women in relation to these two factors is traditionally defined as having to grab what they can before their looks start fading, the problem for men supposedly has more to do with all the sex they will miss out on once they have a wife. Edith Wharton's *The Age of Innocence* is a beautiful story about love, sex, death, choice, law – and carriages – with a man at the centre of the maelstrom. Newland Archer is a bit of a dandy and a total social conformist, who begins the story with some very hokey ideas about marriage. He is engaged to be wed to the supremely naïve May Welland and imagines he will soon be able to fill her mind with whatever he chooses, like a pre-technological Stepford wife: '"We'll read *Faust* together … by the Italian lakes …" he thought, somewhat hazily confusing the scene of his projected honey-moon with the masterpieces of literature which it would be his manly privilege to reveal to his bride.' Unfortunately it turns out that May has a mind of her own, albeit an extremely stiff and conventional one. In fact she turns out to be even more stuck in the norms of her day than he is. Trouble is introduced in the form of May's cousin, the charismatic Countess Olenska, who has suddenly reappeared in New York having left her abominable husband. We are never exactly sure why he's so appalling, but the vague suggestion seems to be that he's been involved in something pervy and weird. It doesn't take Newland long to notice that the countess is a lot more interesting than his wife, but there is the serious problem of propriety. If anything happened between himself and the countess he would become a total social pariah.

Because the rich live in each other's pockets in order to avoid risking meeting the poor, it turns out that everybody in Wharton's novel knows everybody else's business. Newland's wife cunningly manages to get herself pregnant at the precise moment at which he has almost plucked up the courage to tell her he's in love with Madame Olenska. May and all her family gang together to get the countess permanently out of the way. Madame Olenska seems to deal with her fate far more stoically than Newland Archer. While he makes a fuss and complains about what's happening, she can admit that she's in love with him at the same time as being able to do the done thing. This, of course, is because she's been through it all before with the count and likes the idea of some people somewhere behaving decently. If Newland stays with May it enables Madame Olenska to believe that the world isn't a totally awful place. And so she pushes him to do the socially correct thing. '"What's the use?"' asks Newland. '"You gave me my first glimpse of a real life, and at the same moment you asked me to go on with a sham one. It's beyond human enduring." ... There they were, close together and safe and shut in; yet so chained to their separate destinies that they might as well have been half the world apart.' So Newland gets on with bringing up his family, acting like a husband and keeping his trap shut.

Edith Wharton's book came out in 1920 but was set in the 1870s. As the characters age, the world around them changes. When Newland Archer's grown-up son hears the story of his father and Madame Olenska on his mother's deathbed, he can't quite see the big deal. When his father makes a fuss about his knowing, the son tells him not to be 'so prehistoric'. In the 1920s people clearly had the idea that they had a great deal more sexual and romantic freedom than their parents' generation. Newland Archer's tragedy may have appeared to his son as 'a pathetic instance of vain frustration'.

But if it used to be people's fate to suffer their destinies uncomplainingly – sticking with dreary spouses while longing for perkier ones – does the loosening-up of the laws and practices around divorce actually fix it? Is the problem of choice and death really something you can lessen? Or is it just a harsh and ineluctable fact of life? As one single mother recently told me, it was great when she was married to her boorish husband in that she could fantasize about how nice life would be once she finally left him. At last they separated, but the endless rows about childcare, schools and birthday parties carried on. She soon realized that now there was no way out – she was stuck with the guy at least until the children finished university. And, now that they were divorced, there was no imaginary exit.

In terms of how society reacts to separations, we may not be as cool as we like to think we are. When Hanif Kureishi published his book *Intimacy*, a first-person account of a man leaving his wife for a much younger woman, some parts of the London literary world reacted much like Newland Archer's compatriots might have. In Kureishi's case things were complicated by the fact that he'd plainly based his novel on his own real-life experiences. Perhaps if he had quietly walked out and not written about it, it might have seemed more forgivable. Instead he revealed all sorts of painful details about his marriage, and unapologetically documented his excitement about his youthful girlfriend. It seems that separations are allowed these days as long as you don't speak about them. If you honestly try to describe the sorts of selfish, greedy impulses that made it impossible for you to submit yourself to a life of boredom, you suddenly present a serious threat to the nice people.

In 1927 Frederick Lonsdale wrote a comic play called *On Approval*, which was thought to put forward a rather daring premise. If choosing the wrong spouse meant boredom/frustration/fury, then wouldn't it be better if you could have a partner for a trial period before committing to buy? In the story, the forty-year-old widow, Maria, receives a proposal of marriage from her admirer, Richard. Evidently her first marriage was a bit of a trial, and she tells her friend Helen, 'Next time I should like to know a great deal more.' 'But how can you know without marrying him?' asks Helen. Maria's novel idea is that she will spend a month on a remote Scottish island with Richard and make her decision at the end. Helen is concerned about funny business, but Maria assures her that she'll be carrying a revolver (just to make it clear we're not discussing any normal dating-type scenario here). Things become more complicated when Richard's obnoxious friend, the Duke of Bristol, decides to accompany them. And just to make it even worse, Helen also turns up, and all four of them find themselves stuck in the house together. The staff, sensing impropriety, immediately walk out, and the four spoilt

aristocrats are left to fend for themselves. As they get the meas-
ure of each other, things begin to deviate further and further
from the plan. Nonetheless, the story somehow ends up with two
happy couples.

The stage play was remade as a film in 1944, by which time
the idea of a trial period was so ludicrously *un*daring that they
had to set it in the 1890s to get people to accept the notion that it
was all meant to be a bit naughty; going to Scotland with a gun
in your garter was hardly considered raunchy by the tail end of
the Second World War. This echoes the time-slip in Wharton's
novel (also between the early twentieth and late nineteenth
century), which might make us wonder whether there ever really
was an 'age of innocence' or whether it's simply comforting for
people to imagine there was. *Of course* our parents and grand-
parents weren't up to anything – yuck! – *we* invented sex, they
just procreated. Presumably in the 1890s people thought the
same. The gap has to be continuously drawn and redrawn in
order that we can prop up our own repressions concerning our
parents' sexuality. (Of course this is slightly harder to do these
days as our parents may well have been members of the 1960s
and 1970s generations of chronic sexpots. We can attempt to deal
with this by persuading ourselves that the sex *itself* was innocent
and didn't have anything like the filthy emotional consequences
that sex has today.)

In *On Approval*, the two marriages resulting from the Scottish
trip appear to make sense. The nice, calm people end up together,
as do the bolshy, volatile ones. We are presumably supposed to
believe they'll be happier this way, the kind ones avoiding the

horror of being crushed by domineering partners, and the bossy ones getting enjoyment from finally having met their match. Frederick Lonsdale's 'solution' to the problem of morbidity and choice has something of the flavour of the last good fairy in *Sleeping Beauty*: 'I can't undo the spell but I can soften it a bit.' The characters' choices are still binding, but they haven't been made in total darkness. There's therefore some hope that their marriages won't make them quite as unhappy as poor old Newland Archer's.

Till the Surreal Thing Comes Along

So is this still the state of the art where love, sex and commitment are concerned? Try before you buy and hope they weren't putting on an act to trick you? In practice, this appears to be what people actually do, but is it the last word on the subject? In his book *The Century*, Alain Badiou suggests a serious alternative. In his chapter on avant-gardes he tells us, 'The [twentieth] century has been a great century for the vision of love as a figure of truth, which is entirely different from romanticism's fatalist and fusional conception of love.' In other words, in the past you fell madly in love and stuck together in sickness and in health, for better or worse, etc. You went wild with desire, then grinned and bore it until you dropped dead. But in the twentieth century love became something more of an open question. It was no longer about accepting the consequences of it, but about letting it be a more volatile and open-ended state. You didn't have to get stuck with a single notion of what love involved but could allow it to be whatever it seemed to want to be. Badiou formulates his ideas using a passage from André Breton's surrealist text, *Arcanum 17*, in particular the following sentence: 'And I know that the love which at this point counts on nothing but itself does not recover and that my love for you is reborn from the ashes of the sun.'

Badiou is writing about twentieth-century art movements and the ways in which artists managed to make radical breaks with their predecessors. Rather than accepting and repeating received ideas about beauty and form, artists throughout the twentieth century put these very ideas in question in order to rethink what art could be. This sort of revolutionary art activity is discussed in the context of political revolution, raising the question of whether there's any point in rebellions and over-turnings. Is the upset of political revolution ever really justified by the results, or is it ultimately better to knuckle down and do the best you can with what's on offer? Breton and Badiou's answer is that the importance of revolution isn't in its measurable results, but in the act itself. If something has to change, then it's not your job to make sure it changes into something perfect. You just have to change it, and the act of change will almost necessarily be exhilarating. Avant-gardes in art don't seriously aim to 'improve' art in the long run – although they may aim to open things up by toppling a dominant set of ideas. The point in revolution is to access a certain kind of extremely fragile and slippery truth; to stop life becoming a series of empty gestures. The aim isn't to solve the problem once and for all, but to create a space for something to feel somehow real, if only temporarily.

It's possible to see how all these ideas might also apply to love relations – and Badiou refers to 'artists, scientists, militants and lovers' as the century's key avant-garde activists. It's very easy for any love to turn into a set of expected behaviours – they call or text you every day, you have sex three times a week, you never forget to say 'bless you' when your partner sneezes. If one of these things weren't to happen, then it would be a sign that something must be wrong. So you have to keep doing whatever you do in order to sustain the idea that you love each other. Gradually, these acts of love become almost persecutory; if you skip one you're in trouble. You can't do them 'lovingly' any more, in fact you slightly resent them. Or do you resent the other person for insisting on them? In either case, this sort of rigidification of the practices of love becomes a problem in your relationship. If love is just *that*, then it doesn't make you happy. Revolution is called for.

The nature of the revolution is up to you. Do you ditch your partner and get a new one? (And will this new one turn out to be George Bush to your ex's Saddam Hussein?) Or do you revolutionize the activities you perform with the same person? (More like the transition from Picasso to Pollock – stick with paint on canvas, but with a different agenda.) Perhaps you become 'just friends' with your current partner AND try to do everything completely differently with a new one (the Velvet Revolution). In any case, there has to be some kind of (possibly painful) upheaval and things can then continue on a different, fresher course.

'The key issue,' says Badiou, 'consists in thinking love not as destiny, but as encounter and thought, as an asymmetrical and egalitarian becoming, as the invention of oneself.' Love here isn't seen as a choice which one makes and then has to tolerate, but as a series of events or actions in which both parties may be affected or even transformed. As in any revolutionary activity there is the risk of failure and pain but, in love, this may even become a sign that you are taking it seriously. Badiou uses Breton's text to point to a love that has nothing to do with the hefty life-choices faced by the likes of Dorothea Brooke. He is referring to a kind of love that is only fully registered in the incandescent here-and-now of romantic insurrection. A love that isn't obliged to hoover the dishes or water the car (although it doesn't preclude domestic activities so long as they don't become the necessary tropes of a satisfactory life together). In short, precisely the type of love that we mentioned at the beginning of the chapter: a love that is based on pure liking alone.

While Badiou and Breton make it sound extremely exciting and radical – quite rightly – it's not so far from our commonplace contemporary notion that you just have to love who you love, in whatever way you love, and see where it gets you. Badiou doesn't pretend to be saying anything else. He is describing what has become of love as a result of the ideas and practices of the twentieth century. Of course we know it already. The latest answer to the problem of love is uncertainty and pain. Any independent film or literary novel will tell you this. And while mainstream cinema and publishing houses might still shift units on the old notion that happy endings actually exist, that other great contemporary form, the soap opera, endlessly shows us what happens to people as their lives together go on … and on … and on. We watch them split up, make up, have affairs, get over them, come out of the closet, go back into it, and generally deal with whatever other attention-grabbing hurdles their creators can stick in front of them. Soap opera makes it very clear that love is a process rather than a static state.

I Couldn't Help But Wonder …

If French theory isn't to your taste you can always turn to American TV. But what will mainstream culture tell you about love? Of course, there are the endless comforting retellings of fairy-tale happy matches on TV, in films, novels and women's glossy magazines. But there are also popular stories which try to take seriously the shifting impossibility of love. One obvious example would be *Sex and the City*. It certainly looks like the sharp end of contemporary sexual liberation, with episodes focusing on anal sex, non-exclusive relationships, vibrators and threesomes, not to mention the effects of farting in a sexual relationship. Plus it goes into all the emotional complexities that arise from taking an open-minded approach to sex. What sort of impact might watching porn have on your relationship? How will you feel if one of your friends sleeps with your ex? What would it be like to have sex with a gay couple? But is *SATC* actually proposing a different approach to love, or are all the botched attempts and comic disasters simply obstacles on the path to the ultimate goal of a happy marriage? Are we seeing the apex of twentieth-century avant-garde romance, or yet another wheeling out of 'romanticism's fatalist and fusional conception of love'?

Proper *SATC* fans might say it's unfair to take the movie as representative of the phenomenon, that the film is a pathetically sentimental coda to an otherwise serious and honest exploration of modern romance. Still, this is what I'm about to do. I can only justify it by saying that the movie deals explicitly with the problem of love and destiny.

The movie is set four years after the end of the HBO series. Three of the characters are already married to people they met while they were still on TV. The main character, Carrie, is about to get married to her long-term, on/off, super-rich boyfriend, Mr Big. She makes the mistake of getting swept away by extravagant wedding plans, while all Mr Big wants is to be with her without the fuss of a huge, embarrassing consumer-fest. He bolts at the last minute, Carrie freaks out, and they spend the rest of the movie delaying their inevitable reunion. Meanwhile, ex-nympho Samantha is getting fatter and fatter as she attempts to trim her libido to fit the shape of her marriage, Miranda is sulking because her husband (and father of her child) had a one-night stand, and Charlotte is wallowing in domestic bliss with her adopted child and divorce-lawyer spouse. The story concerns the question of what will happen to all these marvellous, attractive, lively women now that they have what all women are supposed to long for: tons of money, swanky handbags and men who want to be with them. Are they actually finding it fulfilling, or not?

There is one strange feature of the movie that I can't resist pointing out. Throughout the film, Carrie Bradshaw appears to be writing her own version of this book, *my* book. Like any author, she suffers and tears her hair over it. She writes the word 'Love …' then deletes the dots, then reinserts them. (I haven't actually done this yet, but I still may.) She gets into bed with Mr Big at night with a medley of all the best love letters in history, from Beethoven, to Napoleon, to Stendhal. (I have done the equivalent of this.) She wonders whether there's anything sensible or useful to be said about love. (Me too, obviously.) The only difference between her and me is that she does most of this in $600 heels. And while the book itself seems a bit lumpen and impossible, life around her continues to be mesmerisingly complex and juicy. Lessons are learned, in droves. In terms of whether these lessons are old-fashioned George Eliot-type lessons or newfangled Badiou-type lessons, it's rather hard to say.

Charlotte's perfect marriage is a kind of after-the-end-of-an-Austen-novel fantasy. This is what living happily ever after is meant to look like. It's so ludicrous and fake that the only way to justify it is to make Charlotte a very pretty android; she is happy because she's sub-human, and her husband is happy because her sub-humanness combines very well with her prettiness. *Lesson one:* if you want a trouble-free relationship, at least one of you might have to be seriously thick.

The other three relationships are slightly messier and more nuanced. Miranda has to choose whether to forgive her husband his sexual indiscretion, and to recognize that she may, in fact, have pushed him towards it. At the same time, he has to forgive her for being such a frigid ball-breaker. In therapy together they manage to dismantle the fixed ideas they have of one another and to recognize each other as human beings (which immediately results in hot sex). You could say that they combine something of the notion of love as a very exciting dialectical activity – resolving their differences through rational discussion and achieving a sexy synthesis – with the older ideal of staying together for the sake of the kids. *Lesson two:* you have to be empathetic and flexible if you are to survive long periods together. Put more simply: don't take each other for granted. A bit obvious, but unarguably very wise.

Samantha has to cope with the fact that she truly loves her husband, but truly hates being married to him. She can try to get the satisfactions she's been missing out on by replacing them with food, but this gets in the way of other satisfactions, like looking good in tight trousers. No amount of couple counselling would be able to make up for the sexual variety she lacks. So she has to choose between denying her sexual appetites or leaving the man she genuinely loves. She chooses to leave, and he appears to take it extremely well. It seems certain that they will remain friends. It also seems possible that they will have much better sex once they are separated. *Lesson three:* genuinely loving (and lusting after) someone and being able to sustain a marriage to them are not at all the same thing. Long-term monogamy isn't the necessary outcome of sincere love. Very Badiou. Excellent!

Last of all there's Carrie and her impracticable relation with Big. No other man will do, but Big keeps flaking out on her. Carrie is a very explicit mixture of the old-fashioned and the modern. She expects her heart to skip beats and stuff, but she doesn't particularly expect 2.4 kids to result from it. She also expects to wear very expensive clothes and eat in very expensive restaurants, so it would make sense for her to expect to pair off with a man with lots of dough. Big is perfect in that he can buy a penthouse flat in Manhattan without having to think about it. And he is also perfect in that he seems as hesitant about love and commitment as she is. (Plus he gives her butterflies.) He's already been married a couple of times and doesn't hold out high hopes for the institution. She can't treat him like an idiot because he's obviously no more of an idiot than she is. The question is whether two such well-matched idiots can work something out between them. This is perhaps the best question two lovers can ever hope to face. How they answer it can only ever be particular to them. They may have to keep thinking up new answers as each idiotic solution will only ever do for a while. But if they are creative they should be able to keep the game up for ages.

Carrie and Big are always reaching points of impossibility in their relationship, then overcoming them. It seems to be what they like doing. They don't act like automatons (like Charlotte) but appear to be sentient beings. Big's anti-marriage stance is a sure sign that he's a proper person. When Carrie falls into acting like a total bridal magazine cliché, he is understandably put off. It's as if the intimate, human dimension of their relationship is being obliterated by an empty cultural ideal. The fact that it makes him nervous is ultimately what makes Carrie love him. But it presents a temporary problem in that it causes him to abandon her in the aisle. This means she has to hate him for a while, then get over him, which only proves to him that she's a mature, independent woman and not a pathetic leech. So now they can get back together, at least until next time.

With Carrie and Big (as well as with Miranda and Steve), *Sex and the City* seems to propose a mid-point between love as destiny and 'a love which counts on nothing but itself'. The very difficult solution it puts forward is somehow to combine the comfort and security of long-term companionship with the exhilarating ambiguity of a here-and-now free from promises or plans. It seems that if it can be done at all it's only with great difficulty, and possibly with the risk of breakages. Both Miranda and Steve and Carrie and Big separate and then get back together. It's as if they have to lose each other in order to find new ways to be together. It brings to mind that other brazenly neurotic American journalist, Mignon McLaughlin (who wrote for *Vogue* in the 1940s), and her famous quote, 'A successful marriage requires falling in love many times, always with the same person.' On the surface, such a pairing may look less idyllic than Charlotte's kitschly impeccable existence, but at least it gives both halves of each couple the space to be a bit more hetero-geneous and divided – a bit more human.

If marriage – or buying a house together, or even just moving in – almost inevitably shakes up one's sense of mortality (this is a choice I'm making for the rest of my life), it can also *be* a kind of death in itself. It's not just that it invokes the question of what to do with one's meagre options, but it may also involve the killing-off of other alternatives. Samantha can't be happy in her marriage because she has to attempt to eradicate a very important part of herself. Lots of marriages seem to demand an almost impossible sacrifice. If we are to live side by side with another person, we may have to deny ourselves all sorts of pleasures. Even if the advantages seem worth it, it might not be easy. And if we feel guilty about our 'inappropriate' desires we may try to hide them, even from ourselves, which might leave us feeling depleted and zombie-like, as if we aren't quite all there. Or it might make us mistreat our partners, as we secretly blame them for our loss. The Carrie–Big/Miranda–Steve model may look a bit wobbly but at least it gives everyone room to breathe. They make mistakes, express doubts, let each other down from time to time. It's very far from perfect. But it does at least seem to allow them to feel that they are continually rechoosing each other, rather than living out their days under the shadow of a rigid and mortifying choice. Which leads us neatly to *Lesson four*: if you take love seriously, you'd better have an open mind.

Perhaps Badiou's proposal, in its purest form – that love should count on nothing but itself – is simply too challenging for most people to bear. For a start it goes against the ways that so many people live. In *SATC*, for instance, real estate is a serious factor in Carrie and Big's decision to marry. This sort of consideration is extremely difficult to avoid. For love to be entirely cut loose from the deadening pragmatics of daily life, daily life itself would need to be entirely rethought. No more private housing for a start (freely usable spaces, like those public bicycles parked around Paris?). Even if one does try to live as far as possible in the heat of the moment, micro-choices will no doubt be generated as each millisecond unfolds. If you feel passionate love for someone *right now*, should you tell them, or will that dictate what happens next? If you let yourself love someone today, will that mean you can't leave them tomorrow? And isn't it important to put the other person first sometimes? To occasionally subordinate your needs and wishes to theirs? How is any relation possible without a certain level of submission? Even the most passionate one-night stand will involve a degree of compromise. Your place or mine? Bedroom or bathroom? On top or underneath? You will somehow have to find ways to reach agreements if you both want to have a good time. And the act of submission itself may even be enjoyable. What could be more tedious and alienating than only ever getting what you want?

But if Carrie and Big can be taken as one example of realistic-revolutionary love, that still leaves the question of what all the other examples might be like. Badiou is pointing us towards myriad forms of love *without* models. We can no more look to *SATC* than we can look to *Middlemarch*. Love, for each of us, might be anything. And while there may be certain things we insist on repeating from relationship to relationship, we will also have our trajectories interrupted by the people with whom we engage. Like characters in our own private soap operas, we can blunder and experiment and make mistakes. And, with luck, keep ourselves and our friends entertained in the process.

6.

Hate That I Love You

What's the relation between love and hate?

♥   ♥

Where we look at love and hate and try to
spot the difference

———————

YOU KNOW THAT WHEN I HATE YOU, IT IS BECAUSE
I LOVE YOU TO A POINT OF PASSION THAT UNHINGES
MY SOUL.

Julie de Lespinasse

When you meet someone who makes you feel something, it may not be immediately obvious exactly what it is. And that's not to mention why on earth they've made you feel it. A bisexual friend once told me that when she met a woman she found attractive she could never quite tell whether she was experiencing envy or desire. If she admired the sharp L of the woman's jawline, did she hate the woman for it, or did it inspire love? If the woman was clever and funny, was it a threat or a draw? Perhaps because this friend was also interested in men, and therefore in the sorts of things a man might like in a woman, it was never a simple matter. If another woman had admirable qualities, did she want to be near her, or to get her out of the way? Or both? And was it something peculiar to her sexuality, or was this sort of thing common in people of all persuasions? If a woman is attracted to a man for his forthrightness and professional power, does she simply want to sleep with him, or to *be* him? Is sleeping with him a way to acquire something of these qualities by proximity? Or perhaps to disempower him? And why do one's feelings for people so often seem to hinge on these single features – a jawline, forthrightness? What do these traits *really* signify?

In the seventeenth century, Spinoza went to work on explaining exactly these sorts of phenomena. Proposition 16, in part III of his *Ethics*, tells us:

> From the mere fact that we imagine a thing to have
> something similar to an object that is wont to affect the
> mind with pleasure or pain, we shall love it or hate it,
> although the point of similarity is not the efficient cause
> of these emotions.

If someone shares certain qualities with someone else about whom we have strong feelings, then these strong feelings may be transferred onto the new person. But the feature in common may have nothing to do with our emotions. Say we used to be in love with a little boy with overgrown hair and a funny name. If in our adult lives we come across someone with these two features we may feel instantly well disposed towards them. This was a fact already noted by Descartes a number of years before Spinoza. He had loved a cross-eyed girl in his youth and was ever since drawn to cross-eyed people. Although he hadn't loved her *for* her crossed eyes, they had since become the emblem of a loveable person. And the same would go for hate: if we are reminded of someone we hate, it may be hard for us to like this poor, innocent stranger with a totally irrelevant feature in common. It's a very nice simple theory, and demonstrably true. But things get more complicated when we are reminded of more than one thing at a time. Proposition 17 tells us:

> If we imagine that a thing that is wont to affect us with an emotion of pain, has something similar to another thing which is wont to affect us with an equally great emotion of pleasure, we shall hate it and love it at the same time.

The same object might share qualities with a number of different predecessors, triggering conflicting emotions in us. We really don't know whether we like it or hate it because it reminds us of so many things. You could say that this is almost bound to be the case in any human interaction. People are made up of so many different things – voice, face, temperament, taste, shampoo smell, etc. – that they're liable to trigger a multitude of disparate associations. It's very unlikely that you would be predisposed either to love *or* hate every aspect of a single person. It stands to reason, therefore, that however much you love someone, there will be something (or things) you loathe about them – and vice versa. It's just a mathematical inevitability. There's also a high chance that you will feel the opposite of what you might expect. Suppose you have a sister whom you love very much. There are things about her that annoy you, but you'd rather not think about them. You meet someone who reminds you of her, but you hate this new person. It's perfect – now you can get on with loving your sister while working off all the hate you feel for her on her stand-in.

To complicate things further, it can't simply be a matter of what we bring to the object, it's also what it brings to us. Some people seem to like us before we've even had a chance to be nice to them (must be our lovely cross-eyes!) while other people treat us like mosquitoes before it's even occurred to us to suck their blood. According to Spinoza, we'll love or hate them back according to whether or not we actually believe ourselves to be the cause of their feelings. In Proposition 40:

> He who imagines he is hated by someone to whom he
> believes he has given no cause for hatred will hate him
> in return.

But if someone hates us for a good reason we'll be inclined to agree with them and hate ourselves too. If they love us for what we see as a good reason – our great personality, our lovely legs – then we will love ourselves too. But if they love us for no apparent reason, then we will love them in return.

Of course this already gives us a lot of variables. What if they love us for no reason but remind us of our evil physics teacher? What if they hate us for a reason but have the spiralling curls of our first love? What if they have the voice of the physics teacher and the hair of the first love and they are drawn to us because they always fall in love with artists/cyclists/blondes? While Spinoza's propositions are brilliantly logical, they can only really show us that love and hate are part of a big, confusing muddle. It may be fascinating to untangle our own reasons for liking or hating another person, but we'll probably never get to the bottom of it. And we really don't have a hope in hell of ever fully understanding what the other person makes of us. Having said that, it can be helpful to bear in mind that a person's reasons for loving or hating us might actually be very little of our business – as the following story clearly shows.

A Spinozistic Fable

A woman's boyfriend told her that he couldn't love her because – at size S (as opposed to XS, or XXS) – she wasn't thin enough. This made her hate herself because, like most women, she thought she ought to be a bit slimmer. You could say this was an unusual example of someone telling someone else the truth about how they saw them. But you could also say he said this because he simply wanted to be cruel; he knew how to tap into her own self-hate and really upset her. And the reason he may have wanted to hurt her was because being loved made him feel too vulnerable.

The man's mother had left the family when he was a small child and he hadn't seen her since. His previous girlfriend had always been on the verge of leaving him, and had cheated on him a number of times. This must have suited him perfectly, as the relationship had lasted seven years. When this beautiful, unsuspecting, slim woman had suddenly walked into his life, promising to love him exclusively, it seems to have made him very anxious. While his previous partner had been just right, never giving him quite enough to attach himself to, this new person might actually expect to be loved in return. And if he loved her, then she might still leave him, and he would be destroyed all over again. So the most important thing was to get rid of his new girlfriend, and maybe also to punish her for being the sort of person who unwittingly threatened to smash up his world.

After the relationship ended, a new twist occurred. It transpired that the man's mother hadn't *wanted* to leave, but had been pushed out by his father and the father's girlfriend. The pain of being ousted from the family home was so great that she'd had a breakdown, which had given the wicked stepmother a legal excuse to keep her away from the kids.

This man hated his mother because she'd ditched him – and quite possibly hated himself for failing to keep her there. But he also loved his mother and, it emerged, she had quite clearly loved him too. The size S woman, by being quite upfront about her affection for him, had presumably reminded him of his adoring mother – and therefore also of his abandoning mother, since they were the same person. Perhaps at the very moment he was starting to feel attached to her, he'd suddenly opted to escape. But because of the hatred he felt for his mother, he'd used a tactic brilliantly designed to punish his girlfriend and make her feel terrible, as if it was all her fault that he was leaving her. (And perhaps to make her hate him back enough to go without a fuss.)

History doesn't record whether the mother was fat or thin, but the stepmother is a certified roly-poly. So what seemed like a heartless insult could in fact be interpreted as the echo of an ancient tragedy that the new girlfriend could do very little about.

Ah, the joys of modern dating.

The Breast of All Possible Worlds

Is it simply the case that the good things and the bad things coexist and you just have to try to keep your mind on the nice bits? This is a neat theory, but it requires you to believe that love and hate are totally separate emotions with very distinct sources, that love and hate simply get shuffled together like a pack of cards and could still be separated out into black ones and red ones if you had the time or the patience. But isn't there something more conjoined about the two emotions? Perhaps they actually somehow produce or feed off each other, and love can actually *cause* hate, as we saw in the unfortunate story above.

If Spinoza's theory points to the precursors for love and hate in each individual's history, psychoanalytic theory takes this idea and pushes it further, showing how our very first interactions dictate how we view the world. In the early part of the twentieth century Melanie Klein was involved in the development of what later came to be known as object relations theory. This is a branch of psychoanalysis that focuses on early relationships and their effects on the developing psyche. The 'objects' referred to are the people and things in the infant's immediate environment, aspects of which may be internalized by the child. As people act on us and affect us, we incorporate some of their qualities and defend ourselves against others – sometimes doing both at the same time.

Klein saw the breast as a very privileged object in the child's universe. On the one hand it was a source of nourishment and enjoyment, but on the other it was a frequent cause of frustration. Either it wasn't there when you needed it, or it was there when you didn't need it, or sometimes, after sucking on it, you felt sick. If a baby was hungry, it would become impossible for it to tell whether the breast was its saviour or its persecutor. The breast certainly appeared to exist in some relation to the gnawing hunger pains but, to the pre-linguistic, pre-logical mind, it was impossible to understand precisely what that relation was. Did the breast cause pain or make it go away? Of course Klein's theories were entirely speculative – who knows what babies really think? – but they made sense of certain phenomena. For instance, why babies sometimes fight against the breast and reject it when they are clearly starving. And why we are so often so horrible to people who are trying to be nice to us. For Klein, the breast was a part-object that came to be split into good and bad components, hence the famous Kleinian notion of the good and bad breast. The 'good' aspects of the breast seem entirely distinct from the 'bad' aspects of it, as if they are two different objects.

This splitting of things into 'good' and 'bad' was fundamental to the organization of the child's psyche, something like the zeros and ones that make up the language of computers – a simple opposition that can be gradually developed and elaborated on in order to perform more complex relations. Throughout its interactions with various entities the child would build up an internal cast of good and bad objects. By identifying and copying it would attempt to include itself in – and act upon – the world around it. It would attempt to understand the external world using mechanisms such as 'projective identification' – i.e. imbuing other people with qualities one possesses oneself. In extreme cases, bad things would be projected out onto other people, while good things would be imaginarily stored up inside oneself (extreme narcissism). Or, equally unfortunately, one might picture oneself full of bad things, with the good things all externalized (severe melancholia). Klein's idea of good mental health involved understanding that one is both good and bad, as are other people. You're bound to be bugged by aggressive and selfish impulses, but that doesn't mean you can't also be generous and altruistic. Other people might be extremely annoying and disappointing sometimes, but they can also be interesting and fun to be around. It's never simply one or the other.

The thing that makes all this slightly different from Spinoza's theory – which nonetheless leads to much the same conclusion – is that the original object (the breast) is the focus of both love and hate. In a sense, Klein tells us that love and hate come from exactly the same place – a place that has everything to do with our relations to other people. As soon as we have strong feelings for an object, the two opposing feelings are liable to be triggered. Will they be nice to us or hurt us? Why do we feel what we feel for them? Do our feelings for them cause us pleasure or pain? The kinds of questions we might have about our relationships dredge up the mysterious codes of our infancy. (And of course, after weaning there are all the other difficult relations to be negotiated: siblings to hit, fathers to be told off by, parents who have frightening and disgusting sex, and all the other horrors of childhood. In short, object relations theory tells us that the average human upbringing is bound to leave us with the odd psychopathic tendency – it's simply a question of degree.)

A Kleinian Tale

The Kleinian idea of 'cure' involves guiding people away from split relations to part-objects, and towards full relations to whole objects. According to object relations theory, you are better when you can deal with the fact that people are all a bit dodgy – and you can love them anyway. The following story shows some of the problems that can spring from expecting your partner to be perfect.

Bina and Max had met at work – both were junior doctors. Max was in a long-term relationship, which ended as he and Bina became closer. Bina was quite certain that she and Max would marry and have children, that they were somehow made for each other. But after six happy months together she became obsessed by thoughts of his previous girlfriend. Had Max really loved her? And if so, why had he left her? If he was capable of leaving someone he loved, then maybe he would leave Bina. Who exactly was this woman he'd spent four years of his life with, then ditched?

Simultaneously, Max somehow caught the virus and began to ask questions about Bina's exes who, it emerged, had mostly been to public school (though she, like Max, was from an extremely poor family and had attended the local comprehensive). Did she have a thing about posh people? In which case, what did she see in him?

The two of them were invited to a charity ball by one of the consultants at the hospital. It was teeming with floppy-forlocked men called Giles. Max, certain that Bina must prefer all the Gileses to him, got very drunk. In the street afterwards he smacked Bina into a wall, pulled her to the ground by her hair and kicked her. When passers-by stopped to help he ran off, but Bina begged them not to call the police. After this, barely a week passed without an explosion. Bina would needle Max with questions about the qualities he admired in women. Who was more attractive, Renée Zellweger or Nicole Kidman? Why? Did he prefer tall or petite women? What had he first noticed about her? What did his previous girlfriend look like? What did he think of so-and-so on reception? If he put a foot wrong – maybe picking out an admirable quality that Bina didn't possess – she would scream at him and sulk and accuse him of not loving her.

Meanwhile Max was slyly transforming himself into a Giles. He bought himself a Barbour jacket and started cycling to work on a folding bicycle. He developed an interest in fishing. He even started to speak differently. It was disturbing to Bina. She suspected him of having a personality disorder. He was also becoming more and more violent, once attacking her with a razor while she was sleeping. He accused her of trying to drive him mad. They became locked in a battle to prove that the other's love wasn't good enough, to the point where it almost seemed that the only way to end it would be for one of them to die. Bina ended up in hospital twice.

Bina was used to violent men, having grown up watching her father hit her mother. He had been shamelessly unfaithful, letting it be known that it was Bina's mother's fault for not being exciting enough to keep him. He kept a supply of pornographic videos in the house and Bina watched them secretly, finding them extremely exciting. Later she said she'd liked looking at them in order to find out what other people enjoyed. She had grown up very sexually adventurous, trying out threesomes, S/M and sex with women. Most of her relationships had ended when she'd become bored, although if it went the other way and a boyfriend left *her*, she'd become obsessed with him almost to the point of stalking.

After a year of vicious fighting Max suddenly left Bina for another woman. She would call and text him obsessively, and let herself into his flat while he was out. She fantasized about hurting him, and about bad things happening to the other woman. Because they lived in a small town, she would hear frequent reports about them, mainly about how unhappy they seemed together. Hearing about their misery was the only thing that made her feel better.

After months of suffering, stalking and crying (and sleeping with a strange array of Gileses) she finally engineered a meeting with Max. He told her he'd really loved her and that he wasn't at all happy with the new woman, but that he couldn't possibly be with Bina because he might unfortunately be compelled to kill her. This seemed to work on Bina – it was somehow okay to be Max's impossible true love. She could get on with sleeping with the Gileses, comparing their various merits and failings, and continuing her private research into what other people (aka her father) might like.

Like the man with the size S girlfriend, Max and Bina clearly had serious doubts about their own loveability. After an initial blossoming of romantic feeling they soon started trying to tear each other down. And the excuse they gave for their thirst for destruction was that the other's love wasn't good enough. Bina felt like she was just another woman for Max, while Max feared he was lacking in relation to Bina's usual type. While they had to fall in love in the first place for any of this to become a problem, the love appeared almost as the necessary preliminary for them to get on with hating each other properly. Bina was an exacting bitch with impossibly high expectations (although Max might be able to play at overcoming this by foolishly aping a type of man he could never possibly become). And Max was a lunkish animal who simply moved from woman to woman without appreciating, or even fully noticing, whoever he was with (and Bina could torment him about this by trying to corner him into saying what made her different from every other woman on the planet – a totally impractical demand). None of which would have mattered if the notion of love hadn't appeared so strongly from the beginning. It had to be there in order to make the hate possible.

It's easy enough to see how some of Bina's identifications might have been at work in all this – she wanted to avoid being her mother by making herself more like one of the women in her father's videos. She may also have wanted revenge on her father for what he did to her mother – and perhaps to experience what her mother experienced at the hands of her father. She was simultaneously acting out a number of roles from her family history. (As was Max presumably, but we don't know what they were.) But both of them also appear to have been floored at the first hurdle by the fact that our love objects are always going to be a bit good and a bit bad. If they had entered into the relationship with the notion that it was possible for something to be 'all good', they had soon set about doing their best to make it 'all bad', as if neither of them was ready to deal with the possibility of something in between.

My Chemical Abhorrence

If all this seems to give too much credence to the psychoanalytic point of view, what can neuroscience tell us about the chemistry of hate? For the moment, it seems, nothing definitive – although there are the beginnings of some interesting hypotheses. As the neuroscientist and philosopher Walter J. Freeman says, 'Virtually nothing is scientifically known about chemistries of jealousy, shame, humiliation, hatred and despair, because the experiences are too painful and too unique in each lifetime to be subject to experimental repetitions and controls.' Still, we know that the peptide hormone vasopressin is linked with aggression, and that it's more present in monogamous prairie voles than in polygamous members of the species. While oxytocin is important in the formation of pair bonds, vasopressin is released when rivals need to be fought off. So aggression understandably plays a special role in species where a pair bond has to be sustained (which means us). Basically, if you love, you may also have to hate. Still, neuroscience has little to say about why aggression is so often suddenly turned onto one half of the pair by the other. Some believe that this may happen in the service of gene distribution – after two to four years it may serve the species better if we go off and find a new mate. In order to do this, it would be best if we stopped liking our partners – and a release of vasopressin would supposedly help us to do this. The same would go for teenagers who need to separate from their parents in order to go off and breed: a well-timed rush of chemicals and, hey presto: 'Mum, you're such a loser.' It all has a slight whiff of *Candide* about it – 'All's for the best in the best of all possible worlds' – but that doesn't mean it's necessarily wrong. You just have to get suspicious when people start talking as though nature actually knows best. There have to be such things as design flaws otherwise evolution wouldn't exist. Just because we are far enough along in the chain to have developed evolutionary theory, it doesn't necessarily follow that we have arrived at a place at which all the problems have been solved.

While vasopressin may be present in situations where our lover makes us mad, it doesn't follow that nature is sensibly advising us to move on. It may equally mean we need to calm down and get over it, or to think about how to handle the situation another way. Where Walter J. Freeman is refreshingly different is in his insistence that human beings are far more complex than most neurobiological theories give them credit for. Taking as a starting point Spinoza's idea that 'man is a social animal', Freeman argues that human brain chemistry is designed to make communication, and therefore society, possible, but that very little can be said for certain about perception and interrelation. There is something absolutely mysterious about what human beings may be trying to do with one another. His key thesis grew out of a series of experiments on rabbit brains where he concluded that it was impossible to predict neural activity – a stable stimulus failed to produce a stable response. What the rabbits' brains did with the information they received was always unique and irregular. This led him to conclude: 'The only knowledge that the rabbit could have of the world outside itself was what it had made in its own brain.'

But if each brain is unlike any other, then how do we bridge the solipsistic gulf between ourselves and other people? Chemicals like oxytocin and vasopressin may be important in helping us organize relationships, but they can't dictate how those relationships will go. Each brain has to constantly dream up its own responses. While we might be subject to chemical attractions and repulsions, we have to make something up to make sense of them. So, in a sense, what we need is precisely *more* silly love songs – and art-house movies and Mills and Boons and gold-leafed pictures of people kissing and multi-media art installations and sonnets. If we are to coexist and procreate we are, between us, going to have to come up with some pretty good models for how it should be done.

Hate Story

If we need to tell ourselves stories about love, we equally need narratives around hate. Barbara Cartland is perhaps the queen of hate-to-love. Her novels frequently show a young girl overcoming her dislike for a prickly, boorish man – and finally falling head-over-heels in love with him. But love-to-hate is also a big theme in popular culture. Lily Allen's first album, *Alright, Still*, was full of hate songs about an ex-boyfriend. In *Shame for You* she imagines getting her brothers to beat him up. In *Not Big* she insults his performance in bed. The songs are excellently unapologetic about her bad feeling towards the person she used to like. There's no point wondering why on earth she didn't help her poor boyfriend by telling him how better to please her in the sack. The idea of the song is simply to reduce him to a pulp to get her own back for whatever blows to her narcissism he dealt her. It's not so strange. It's just that Lily Allen has made pub conversation into an art form. Of course if someone has made you feel absolutely terrible about yourself then it can be nice to return the favour.

But, as with Bina and Max, we wouldn't have to hate the person so much if there hadn't been the hope or possibility that we might love them equally intensely. It seems that once this hope of love has been woken up, then it's very hard to put it back to sleep again. Lily Allen's *Littlest Things* is a really sweet love song about the beginning of a relationship, a perfect counterpoint to the viciousness of the other lyrics. As the laws of physics teach us, energy can't be lost, it simply transforms into something else. If love is invoked then disappointed, it has to turn into something – and hate makes for a very straightforward conversion. To get from love to 'quite liking' takes a little longer, as the intensities of the emotions are not the same. This would perhaps be akin to the conversion of light into heat – the brighter, the hotter. If someone wants to get from incandescent to lukewarm they're going to involve some sophisticated mechanisms (thermo-acoustic cooling?), or leave some time to radiate – and meanwhile you just have to hope they don't write any songs about you.

In the film *Fatal Attraction* the two main characters experience an immediate and extreme pull towards one another. Dan Gallagher's wife and child are away for the weekend when he takes the opportunity to have a brief fling with Alex Forrest, a woman he's bumped into twice via work. While it's often been referred to as an AIDS-era movie that warns against the perils of casual sex, there is something very uncasual about what happens between them. The sex on the first night is pretty rampant, but the dog-walking next day seems semi-domestic – despite being a little too much fun. But when Dan falls over and appears to have a heart attack Alex is distraught. Not only might she have a lot of explaining to do in the hospital, it's just not nice to meet someone you really get along with and then to see them suddenly drop dead in front of you. Luckily, it turns out that Dan is joking. Alex is furious. She tells him her father died in similar circumstances when she was a child. Dan is mortified at having played such a stupid joke on her and apologizes, to which she basically responds by saying, 'Ha ha! Got you back. My dad's fine.' There's a moment of excruciating awkwardness where they both notice how capable they are of upsetting each other. But at the same time it becomes apparent that they really don't know each other at all, and therefore have no way of telling what's real and what's made up.

Later in the film it transpires that Alex's father really did die of heart failure, and this goes a small way towards explaining why she is so nuttily fixated on Dan. Not only might this experience make you grow up a little off-kilter (provided it was backed up by other difficult circumstances), but it may also make you attach yourself to married men with kids who appear to die and then suddenly spring back to life again. The relief and happiness she must have felt at Dan's resurrection is perhaps the correlative to the fury she felt when he had to leave her and go back to his family. How could he turn out not to be dead, but then go and abandon her anyway? In Spinozistic terms, Dan must certainly have reminded her of her dad, causing her to love him, even though 'the point of similarity was not the efficient cause of these emotions'. By playing dead, Dan made Alex's love for him inevitable. But he has a big house and a kid and a really nice wife and mutual friends, etc., so not enough has been triggered in *him* for him to give all that up for her. So he leaves Alex and goes back to his life, while she has to find some way of dealing with the incandescent love that's been fired up in her.

The question the movie-makers were confronted with was whether Alex would ultimately turn her hate onto herself or others. Does she believe she gave Dan cause to hate her or not?

The first serious sign that things are really not okay comes when she slashes her wrists. You could say that she turns her hate onto herself at this point, although the slit wrists seem to function more like Dido's tears; she wants to demonstrate to Dan how much his vanishing matters to her rather than actually end her life. But later on she turns her hate onto Dan, telling him in a tape-recorded message that he's a 'cocksucking son of a bitch'. Next, famously, the rabbit gets it. But at the very end the film-makers seem to have been confused about what Alex should do with her build-up of bad feeling. In the original finale she commits suicide and makes it look like Dan killed her. In this way she manages to punish herself for her own unloveableness, as well as punishing Dan for not loving her. She also presumably manages to hurt Dan's perfect wife and family by exposing him and perhaps putting him in prison. But American trial audiences didn't like it. They wanted to see Dan and his goody-goody wife get revenge for poor Alex's attack on their apple-pie family. So, against the advice of a number of psychiatrists, and the wishes of Glenn Close who was playing Alex, the ending was re-shot to give us the awful bath-drowning and wifely shooting scene with stupid contact lenses. Only Japanese audiences – who are apparently more inclined to see suicide as an honourable solution – were treated to the rightful *Madame Butterfly* finish.

While the film has been criticized for being anti-feminist and sexually conservative – and who's to argue? – it's also a very brilliant depiction of the parity of love and hate. There's no need to ask why Alex does what she does. Of course she's totally psychotic, which makes her do it worse than most of us would, but it's perfectly understandable that she should feel pretty wild when her love is inflamed and Dan's isn't. Much has been made of her sartorial switches from all white to all black; like a light bulb spilling its heat into a suddenly dark room, she has to find something to do with her energy.

Hate Objects

Approximately half of all female homicide victims in the UK are killed by a partner or an ex, as are 8 per cent of murdered men. Home Office statistics tell us that 116 women and 32 men were killed by partners or exes in the year 2001–2. In America roughly a quarter of all homicides are committed by intimates. In France in 2003, when the rock star Bertrand Cantat killed his actress lover Marie Trintignant, half the country apparently leapt to his defence, calling it a *crime passionnel* as opposed to a common-or-garden murder. Although he'd battered her into a coma with his own bare hands, he defended himself in court by saying that it was: *'Un accident, une folie. Mais pas un crime.'*

Looked at like this, falling in love is clearly dangerous. Some of these killings come after years of abuse. Lots of them happen when the victim tries to leave the relationship. What often gets lost in all the bloodthirsty horror of these stories is how much the killer may 'love' the victim. In an article published in the 1980 issue of the *Journal of Contemporary Psychotherapy*, Dr George R. Bach argued against the stereotype of the vicious sadist, presenting a portrait of a typical spouse-killer as a desperate romantic. In a series of interviews with convicted killers he observed that both men and women often showed great commitment to their marriages and resented their spouses for not displaying the same levels of devotion. Many of them seemed to have enormous expectations of the joys that love might bring them, entering into marriage with totally unrealistic ideas about the other person's capacity for sacrifice, tolerance and understanding. The victim was seen as a 'spoiler' – they'd gone and ruined everything by being unfaithful, cranky or just a little dissatisfied.

In his discussion of the sort of love that can take place between a patient and their analyst, Jacques Lacan comes up with the phrase, 'I love you, but, because inexplicably I love in you something more than you – the *objet petit a* – I mutilate you.' This formulation could equally apply to any couple. Person A loves Person B for reasons that Person B may have no understanding of, or control over. Person B seems to contain something that Person A values, although they have no idea what it is. Lacan's *objet petit a* has a lot in common with Melanie Klein's part-object. While it might arouse desire, it also opens up a very high likelihood of frustration and disillusionment. Person A can't access the object in Person B, largely because *it isn't actually there*. Person B's crossed eyes may suggest to Person A that they also contain all sorts of other valued qualities – kindness, loyalty, whatever. But maybe they don't. They may even wonder why Person A keeps hanging round them, gazing at them and generally getting under their feet. Lacan referred to it as 'the object cause of desire' – desire is somehow set in motion by the presence of this feature. As with Spinoza's 'thing which is wont to affect us', if we perceive another person as possessing this object, we may find ourselves trying to access it through them. The problem is that they are likely to be totally unaware of what it is that we seem to find in them. Perhaps they would rather be loved for something else. (Which brings to mind Bina's tormented question: 'What is it that you love about *me*?', and her near certainty that she wasn't loved for the thing she wanted to be loved for.)

Slavoj Žižek has discussed Lacan's *objet petit a* in the context of science fiction. In films like *Invasion of the Body Snatchers* or *Children of the Damned* a town is invaded by an evil force that takes over the minds and bodies of its inhabitants. The protagonists have to be able to spot the small signs which distinguish the possessed from the non-possessed. These may be anything from a physical feature (spooky eyes) to a particular way of understanding the world (the glazed contentment of the Stepford wives). This trait marks the bearer out from 'normal' people – and generally means you'd better watch out for them. When we meet someone and fall in love, then this person too is somehow distinguished from the rest of humanity. They may seem to contain something that other people don't – or to lack the annoying features that other people possess. We may not be immediately able to say what it is about them that separates them off from others, but we know it's there. They are different. We may try to explain it to ourselves using generic 'good qualities' in order to obscure the thing about them that we *really* like. We tell ourselves they're kind and funny, while what really holds us in thrall is their awful teeth. This thing or object that singles them out is very likely to be something they don't value in themselves. Like Spinoza says, it's 'not the efficient cause'— it's a nothing, a by-product, a flaw; certainly not a sensible reason to love someone.

Problems start when the rest of the person doesn't live up to the promise of this attribute. At our most illogical, we may have the unconscious idea that, because their gums are receding and their teeth are lined up like a dilapidated Victorian cemetery, then it necessarily follows that they will provide us with all the comforts and satisfactions we associate with their dentally deficient predecessor. It soon becomes apparent that their teeth and their way of being are two totally different matters. Bad teeth don't *always* equal good character; it may be a case of mistaken identity. It's not the teeth we're after, but something else. The teeth may be the *cause* of desire, but they don't actually give us anything in themselves. As Žižek explains, 'What Lacan calls the *objet petit a* is … the unfathomable X on account of which, when we confront the object of our desire, more satisfaction is provided by dancing around it than by making straight for it.' If we genuinely believe that the person possesses the object, and that we can access it through them, then the result is very likely to be injury. The fact is that they don't contain it, we simply attribute it to them. The object is the thing *beyond* the bad teeth or the crossed eyes. This 'something in you more than you' may have very little to do with you (until, of course, you find yourself being mutilated in the name of it). So Žižek is saying that you get a less deadly, more enjoyable result if you hedge around the idea that the person *might* possess *something* of the qualities you're after than if you brutally insist on their being the person you want them to be.

The tragedy of spouse-killing is often that the 'thing' the murderer loves isn't their partner at all, but the trace of another person that's accidentally emerged in this new place. The rest of the loved one has to be abolished due to their utter difference from the object they appear to contain. The more idealization that takes place in the beginning, the further they have to fall – the gap between the promise offered by the object and the rest of the person is too great. It seems that if you want to love someone without feeling compelled to chop them up, you need to bear in mind that they are probably not who you think they are. Whatever it is that you love about them is really none of their business. You are different, they are different – two independent brains trying to dream up a relation. More silly love songs indeed. And perhaps some silly dancing to go with them.

While Spinoza, Klein and Lacan are all saying different things, if there's an overall message you can extract from the three of them, it's that you should try to lower your expectations where your loved ones are concerned. Not only are they other than you think they are, but no one could ever be all good. At least if you expect them to be flawed and totally at variance with your ideals then you might be able to enjoy the things that you just happen to like about them – and not hate them for failing to be a perfect copy of some imaginary person you carry around in your head. Being aware of this might also make you more tolerant in the other direction, when your lover becomes frustrated with you for not being the person they want you to be. It's not (just) that they are a vile despot, but that they are trying to match the things they find in the world to the unique and bizarre constructions in their own minds.

In his supremely intelligent film *The Love Guru*, Mike Myers' character – Guru Pitka – has come up with a number of trade-marked wordplays and acrostics, which he proudly presents during his star-studded PowerPoint presentations at his ashram in India. 'Intimacy' becomes 'into me I see' and 'guru' is broken down into its constituent letters: 'G.U.R.U: Gee, you are you!' In spite of being a total maniac, he manages to cure everyone's love problems, including his own. Although his catchphrases are obviously ludicrous and comical, they are also ingenious and clever. With his super-glib slogans he crystallizes two very important ideas: in love, you'd better be wise to your own agenda – you should know what peculiar expectations you bring to the equation ('into me I see'). And you need to allow yourself to be surprised by the other person's being – don't constantly expect them to conform to your image of them ('Gee, you are you!'). If both halves of a couple can do this, then there's some hope it won't all end up at the morgue.

7.

Only You

Is monogamy a good idea?

♥   ♥

In which we look at the politics of love, and take tips
from the birds and the bees concerning infidelity

LOVE IS BLIND, BUT MARRIAGE RESTORES ITS SIGHT.
Georg Christoph Lichtenberg

The United States has the world's highest divorce rate. More than half of all marriages end within ten years. The UK follows closely behind, with Korea in third place. China and India are catching up, with divorce rates as much as doubling in a single decade. In Germany there is what's become known as a 'divorce economy', with divorce-themed bars, clubs and magazines becoming so popular that it's started to look like an attractive lifestyle choice. Statistics tell us that, in Britain, a couple gets married every 2 minutes and 42 seconds. Divorces take place at the rate of one every 3 minutes and 24 seconds. Of the marriages, 41 per cent are first-timers, while 59 per cent are remarriages. During these marriages roughly 60 per cent of the men and 40 per cent of the women will cheat. (Statistics here are unreliable as the subjects of the research are notorious liars.) Slightly over half of the marriages will fail. The average cost of a British wedding is £16,000. You can build a well in Africa for £100.

All this seems to me to invite a number of questions:

1. Why the hell does anybody do it?
2. Why the hell would anybody do it *twice*?
3. And who the hell gets married at 4.47 in the morning?

There has always been a question as to whether there's anything natural about marriage. On the one hand there's the Platonic myth of the 'other half' – the person who completes you and without whom you could never be happy. And then there's something more along the lines of Friedrich Engels' notion of the 'conjugal partnership of leaden boredom known as "domestic bliss"'. According to some, marriage (or a committed, monogamous relationship) is something human beings seem naturally inclined towards, while for others, it's a dreadful cultural imposition that we'd be better off without. In the words of Engels, '[Monogamy] was not in any way the fruit of individual sex-love. … The Greeks themselves put the matter quite frankly: the sole exclusive aims of monogamous marriage were to make the man supreme in the family, and to propagate, as the future heirs to his wealth, children indisputably his own.'

Engels argues that monogamy has nothing to do with sexual jealousy and possessiveness – and even less to do with the endless satisfaction that supposedly comes from finding one's true soulmate – and everything to do with private property. If property belonged to the group or community then it didn't matter who got their hands on it after you died – it wasn't your problem. But once people got it into their heads that they actually *owned* stuff then they started to worry about what would happen to it when they weren't around to keep an eye on it any more. A good way to sustain the illusion that there was any point in acquiring *things* was to hand your hard-won possessions over to a son who would keep your name, and your best gear (and maybe have your nose). Of course he had to *actually* be your son otherwise you wouldn't get the sense that you'd solved the problem of mortality so deftly. So you needed to make sure your woman didn't sleep with anyone else, and having some kind of public agreement to that effect seemed to be a good way to bring it about. Everybody would know she was all yours and steer clear. Of course they would.

Trouble and Strife

While marriage can be a great source of pain and difficulty for both sexes, the first big critiques of the institution were made on behalf of women. Almost a hundred years before Engels, Mary Wollstonecraft wrote *A Vindication of the Rights of Woman* (1792), in which she laid into the way women were under-educated, patronized and given little more to hope for in life than a husband who would support them. She objected to the manner in which the feminine character was trained, or deformed, according to the notion that ladies were gentle, sentimental, delicate, self-absorbed, fascinating (until they turn thirty) and a little bit thick. All this, of course, was presented as an undeniable fact of nature rather than as an extremely long-term and effective brainwashing programme. She thought that if women could ignore the supposedly complimentary side of the assault – 'You're so quaint and pretty, I could put you on my mantelpiece and completely ignore you!' – then they might get out from underneath it enough to see what a cunning scheme it was. Wollstonecraft believed that by playing dumb (while actually being quite wily) in order to attract a husband, women were selling themselves short. This wasn't their fault, it was just their best option in a world stacked against them. She says, 'Strength of body and mind are sacrificed to libertine notions of beauty, to the desire of establishing themselves – the only way women can rise in the world – by marriage. And this desire making mere animals of them, when they marry they act such as children may be expected to act.' In other words, for women, marriage and idiocy are inextricably linked. Her solution to this wasn't to say, 'Let's forget about marriage and do our own thing', but to suggest that women would make much better wives and mothers if they were given equal rights to education. She compares the pathetic feminine state to a localized gangrene that nonetheless affects the entire body. Not only is it bad for women to try to turn themselves into large fur-less pets – quite decorative to have around, and prepared to let you stroke them in return for food – it's also bad for men. According to Wollstonecraft both sexes would be happier if marriage took place on an equal footing.

While keeping women uneducated in order to maintain power over them is not a practice one would want to return to, Wollstonecraft seems to have been wrong about the beneficial impact of education on male/female relations. Far from making women more informed and interesting companions, it seems to have made women less easily satisfied. Among college-educated couples, 90 per cent of divorces are initiated by women.

In *The Subjection of Women* (1869) John Stuart Mill and Harriet Taylor Mill adopt a view similar to Wollstonecraft's. They point out that women are faced with a kind of Hobson's choice: marriage or nothing, and that once a woman has entered into marriage she ceases to have any rights. As they say, 'No slave is a slave to the same lengths, and in so full a sense of the word, as a wife is. Hardly any slave, except one immediately attached to the master's person, is a slave at all hours and all minutes.' And to make it worse, they are even supposed to *like* it. Like Wollstonecraft, the Mills see women as having been coerced into a completely artificial state of passive 'femininity' to the point where it's no longer possible to say anything about what a woman *is*, or may be capable of, because women's 'true natures' have been so successfully squashed out of existence. The marriage laws were set up entirely in men's favour, with women granted no agency because they were thought to be too dumb and flower-like to deserve it. The legal state of marriage made it possible for men to be as horrible as they liked to women – to hit them, take away their children and have them locked up in institutions for not playing along – and it was just luck if you found yourself a husband who chose to be nice to you. In this respect they go further than Wollstonecraft and suggest some modification to the marriage laws in order to let women with dodgy husbands get themselves out of a bad situation. But generally all three are in agreement that marriage in itself is potentially a good thing, so long as it's more evenly weighted.

And this is where Engels came in. Fifteen years later, in *The Origin of the Family, Private Property and the State*, Friedrich Engels launched a much more ferocious attack on the institution of marriage. Not only was it a pathetic means of clinging on to property and a particularly vicious form of slavery, it was also a source of widespread unhappiness, an inevitable cause of hypocrisy and a terrible bore for all concerned. He refers to 'that compound of sentimentality and domestic strife which forms the ideal of the present day philistine'. It's not just women but men, too, who have to be stupid to marry. He certainly put his money where his mouth was and never married his partner, Mary Burns. While the position of women was at the centre of his tirade, he didn't believe that by simply sending them to school and letting them divorce in cases of domestic violence you would be solving the problem. It went deeper than that – monogamous marriage was a symptom of the unjust and unhappy way in which society was structured. The accumulation of private wealth and the passing-on of property to biological heirs meant that women had to be subjugated to, and policed by, their husbands. This led to the situation described by Wollstonecraft and the Mills – because men couldn't physically be there to watch their wives, they had to use a combination of law, myth and conditioning to keep them in their lowly places. But the problem of property came first, making the entire marriage scam necessary — therefore it was going to take more than a bit of co-education to bring the whole edifice down. One of Engels' ideas was that, by opening the world of work to women, the structure of male/female relations would be forced to change. He argued: 'It will be plain that the first condition for the liberation of the wife is to bring the whole female sex back into public industry, and that this in turn demands the abolition of the monogamous family as the economic unit of society.' All of which sounds great until you remember that the first half of the plan has in fact taken place without the second part getting much of a look-in. Women now go out to work *and* continue to do most of the housework and childcare. The last thing a slave needs is a day job — no wonder the smart ones leave. (Not that divorce solves the problem of housework, it just means you don't have to do it with gritted teeth.)

While Engels could be said to have lived admirably according to his doctrine, you might also say that he didn't exactly push the boat out and set up a sex commune. He basically went in for a fairly standard form of relationship. Of course that's his choice and it would hardly be reasonable to criticize him for it. But his book seems to open up a number of possibilities concerning the future of relationships. If marriage is a miserable arrangement that makes wives sad and pathetic, and husbands frustrated and liable to visit prostitutes (another of his key criticisms of marriage is that it implicitly demands 'monogamy *for the woman only*'), then what would be more likely to make people happy? One option is that people form larger and more flexible family groups involving non-exclusive pairings. If everyone was less fussy about whose kid was whose then maybe they could work better, share better and no longer be imprisoned by a stupid cultural ideal that placed ludicrous and unnatural restrictions on their libidos. People could have multiple partners without guilt, and openly behave more like they do in secret. While Engels doesn't put it quite so explicitly, he hints at this sort of set-up in his references to pre-civilized societies, before everyone got grabby and individualistic. He refers to the stage of savagery where group marriage was the norm, and then to an intermediate stage, which he calls barbarism, where 'pairing marriage' (something more like serial monogamy) was practised. This latter idea is something he clearly holds out more hope for. If dishonesty is a problem in most marriages (you have to pretend to be happy when you're not, you have to pretend to be faithful when you're not), then something more easily dissolved might be a solution; if you get too miserable you can leave rather than lie.

But in case this makes it sound like Engels thought it was okay to be romantically slapdash, he seems to suggest that this less absolute kind of pairing marriage might actually lead to more serious and committed relationships than old-school, of-course-I-love-you-darling arrangements. If the problem with law-enforced, economically underpinned relationships is that they get in the way of more subtle human interactions, causing people to bullshit and disrespect each other, then a lawless pairing, guided by pure sexual, romantic or intellectual preference might open the way for a more interesting exchange. And one of the results of this might be a *truly* monogamous relationship: a fairly agreed-upon, exclusive arrangement on both sides. Engels states as fact that 'sexual love is by its nature exclusive' and that 'marriage based on sexual love is by its nature individual marriage' and predicts that the removal of legal and financial incentives is more likely to make men monogamous than women polyandrous.

But still, he concedes, it's impossible to know what the people of the future will decide. Of course, for Engels, the people of the future meant the people benefiting from the overthrow of capitalist production. For better or worse, there aren't many of these people around. However, gentler divorce laws and the widespread practice of serial monogamy seem to suggest that, at least in the field of sexual relations, things have gone his way. The question is, does it actually make us happier? Or is the kind of serial monogamy we practise yet another symptom of modern capitalism? (Although, as we've said, this position is becoming harder to argue in the face of recent anthropological studies.) When we get sick of the old one we shop around for a new one, feeling ever more alienated and lost in the process.

Lying, Cheating Bushtits

Wollstonecraft, the Mills and Engels all seem to be nursing the charming idea that if you remove a couple of unfortunate cultural constraints then you make way for the true nature of human beings – and that this will necessarily be a good thing. While it would be ungrateful and foolish for any contemporary woman to suggest that she hadn't been done a very great favour by the people before her who made it possible for her to go to college, vote, have sex for pleasure and do interesting work, it may also be fair to say that shifting the balance of power isn't a complete solution to the problem of human misery. It would also be reasonable to point out that the so-called natural world is mainly ordered around the notion that you have to be a bit tough and cunning if you want to breed. There are bribes, lies, fights and pay-offs everywhere. Girl birds go out with boy birds because they have good nests. A female monkey may choose a mate according to his capacity to supply food. Getting one's hands on the good stuff isn't a uniquely human obsession (although inventing complex global systems whereby some people get to gorge off the backs of other people's starvation is, admittedly, particular to our species).

Of course humans are unique animals in that we develop all sorts of sophisticated ways in which to overcome the limits of nature – we fly food around the world so we can eat strawberries any time, freeze our eggs, cut bits off and add bits on, and pull all sorts of tricks in order to live – and mate – for bloody *ages*. You can say it isn't really sensible to look at what our genetically closest primates do and expect to uncover our lost natural essence – we are *totally* different. But you can also say that when chimps look after one another's offspring, or when wildebeests herd together in the hope that the crowd will save them from lions, or when ants build underground colonies, they too are using clever techniques to save themselves from nature. Even plants do it – they grow tasty fruits that get carried off, or develop ingenious aerodynamic seed pods so that rival trees don't sprout too near. Nature and artifice can't really be distinguished: nature *is* artifice – a series of clever tricks to delay death.

So, where might monogamy fit into all this? Is it a completely phoney human construct? Does it have a place in the natural world? Or is what we call the 'natural world' just a series of phoney constructs? Are there animals that are faithful? And, if so, what function might their fidelity serve?

For a large part of the last century it was widely upheld that 7 per cent of mammals and 90 per cent of birds were monogamous. In the case of birds the theory was that because of the egg situation there needed to be two of them around to keep an eye on things – one could go and get food while the other sat around on the nest; the eggs would be safe and the mum wouldn't starve. This suited the males as well as the females because it meant their genes could be passed on. It was worth sticking around and doing a bit of domestic labour if it preserved your DNA. (The birds had it all thought through.) Some birds kept this up for an entire breeding season, after which they parted company. Some did a couple of batches of eggs in a single season, but with different partners, each of whom they were faithful to until the chicks flew the nest. And some, like swans and bald eagles, mated for life. People were delighted by the idea that monogamy existed in nature and swans were widely celebrated for their fine, upstanding ways. (And to cap it all, swans are elegant and well suited to advertising the principle of exclusive romantic love.)

The problem was that it all started to come unravelled in the 1990s with the advent of genetic fingerprinting. As soon as scientists started stomping through the countryside swiping DNA samples it transpired that there was actually a lot of perfidy going on in the avian world. While the 'You nip out while I mind the kids' style of nesting was great for warding off predators and staying fed, it also provided plenty of opportunities for infidelity. (Or extra-pair copulation – EPC, as it came to be known. They had to abbreviate the term due to its total ubiquity.) In some bird species it was observed that as many as 65 per cent of their offspring were not fathered by their official mate. And the females sought out EPCs just as aggressively as the males. One species after another were discovered to be playing away. Even swans. Nature magazines were full of it. After a while your research only became newsworthy if you could discover an incidence of fidelity in a bird. Some kestrels were found to have kept themselves in check for a whole season. A few bushtits were discovered to have nests full of same-father chicks (although they tended to switch partners as soon as child-rearing was over, sometimes bringing the new mate in to help with the chicks while the old mate was still around). Birds went from being the great exemplars of natural monogamy to being just as duplicitous as the rest of us.

And mammals have fared no better. There were gibbons, those famous lifetime monogamists for whom everyone held out high hopes: they're quite like us, and if they can do it so can we. It was generally agreed that gibbons were only monogamous because the females were so antagonistic towards one another that they had to live part apart, making it difficult for the males to be unfaithful due to purely geographical limitations. Still, it was something. Like humans, gibbons have a long pregnancy and period of infant dependency. The females need a male around to defend their territory while they are nursing. For gibbons, territory equals food. So females chase off other females in order to defend their food and semen supply. And males don't mind being controlled in this way because they too get to eat and breed. (Sound familiar?)

Then came the blood tests and the inevitable discovery of EPCs. Gibbons were at it too. Twelve per cent of gibbon sex was estimated to be 'extra-marital'. It suits the males because they get to spread their seed, and it suits the females because it encourages sperm competition. It also gives them access to bigger, stronger males than the one they have at home. So gibbons are faced with the sticky problem of deciding whether to keep a close eye on their partners, therefore losing the opportunity to cheat themselves, or to sneak off and swing with other gibbons, thereby leaving their mate unguarded. We may fret about the Internet opening up new opportunities for married people to mess around, but monkeys manage just fine without it. In fact cheating is such an issue in the gibbon world that the females have supposedly developed desperate strategies to prevent it. On observing the sexual habits of gibbon couples, a number of scientists hypothesized that the females would on occasion shag their mates senseless in order to deplete their sperm supply and therefore stop them straying. A magazine article I read recently that promised tips on how to 'affair-proof' your relationship managed to waffle its way across three double spreads without a single reference to this excellent idea.

As a result of all this, scientists had to break the concept of monogamy into various categories. In place of the fictitious notion of animals getting together and living happily ever after they came up with the ideas of social monogamy, sexual monogamy and genetic monogamy. Social monogamy (as can be seen in many human marriages) refers to monogamy-on-the-surface. The couple act like a perfect pair of homemakers – and then dash out and grab whatever they can get. And, just like most humans, if they catch their partner in the act they make a fuss, chasing off the intruder and preferably hurting them in the process. (I haven't so far found any studies of avian sulking, but maybe there are some out there.) Sexual monogamy means that the couple really do only have sex with one another. This is extremely rare. And last of all there is genetic monogamy, which means only breeding with one partner. (This is perhaps the sort of monogamy that people like Bill Clinton are into.)

Of course most animals don't bother with monogamy at all. Some species, most notably bonobos – our closest relatives – openly have as much sex as possible. They go in for male-to-male and female-to-female couplings and use sex in a number of ways that have little directly to do with breeding – as a form of greeting and as a means of resolving conflicts. They also kiss, with tongues.

So what is the evolutionary advantage of pretending to be faithful? Is there one? The obvious answer is that it covers two bases. On the one hand you get the close bond that makes certain forms of child-rearing possible, and on the other you get the genetic diversity that supposedly promotes species survival. So having your cake and eating it may be the most efficient way to sustain life.

Alone With You

But we are not like other animals. We write love poems, cry over soppy movies and listen to Heart FM. And as much as we may suffer in long-term relationships, we are just as prone to suffer without them. A lot of us seem to like monogamy. Or at least we like the idea that our partner is faithful to us. The last thing most of us want to hear when we meet someone we like is, 'You're great, but we can still sleep with other people, can't we?' (Of course there are plenty of people who want to hear precisely this, but they can have a special chapter of their own.) Monogamous marriage clearly continues to have a place, despite the fact that it is biologically unnatural, statistically unlikely, and often not much fun.

Psychologists often explain this by saying that we begin life as the almost exclusive focus of our mother's attention. But all too quickly she weans us and boots us out into the world. Maybe we are replaced by a sibling, maybe she goes back to work, or maybe she just gets bored with reading *The Cat in the Hat* and finds something better to do. We go about our lives, trying to make the best of this terrible blow to our narcissism, until, one day, we meet some nice person who promises to put us at the centre of their universe. We're back in the top spot. It's great. We want to stay there this time, so we get married, buy a house and become completely gluey and dependent.

According to this narrative there is something natural and inevitable about marriage – it promises to return us to an original, happier state of being, before we had to deal with disappointment and loss. But if marriage is such a great idea from a psychological point of view, why does it so often go wrong?

Freud took issue with the way in which society forbade young people from experimenting with sexuality and promised that it would all come right when they finally got hitched. The guilt and repression that built up around the subject of sex were supposed to dissolve the minute the couple signed a piece of paper. When this didn't happen it led to a situation where husband and wife became disappointed with one another, stopped having sex and ended up every bit as miserable as they'd been before, if not more so. The solution was either to have an affair or to succumb to a neurotic illness. Neurosis was a response to the restrictions placed on the libido by society. Maybe you developed a permanent headache, chronic depression or a phobia. If you couldn't do what you wanted, you got sick. And the only thing you were allowed to want was to have penetrative sex with your spouse. As Freud put it in *'Civilised' Sexual Morality and Modern Nervous Illness*, 'A girl must be very healthy if she is to be able to tolerate [marriage]'. The main difficulty was that marriage was supposed to provide a complete answer to the complex questions of love and sex. One person had to cover the whole business for the rest of one's life. But that person also brought with them all their wishes, repressions, preferences and hang-ups. The idea that you could get lasting emotional and sexual satisfaction from someone just as flawed and erratic as you are was unlikely. But society dictated that you should.

Still, Freud's answer wasn't simply that we should loosen up the rules (although he was obviously in favour of tolerance and open-mindedness). He criticized the communists for their idealistic notion that if you abolished private property and the family you would cure mankind of hostility and ill-will. In *Civilisation and its Discontents* Freud says, 'Aggressiveness was not created by property. It reigned almost without limit in primitive times, when property was still very scanty.' Aggression is an unavoidable human feature. It's always there. Love itself only exists in relation to aggression – it's a trick to help us overcome it. (This is something with which the evolutionary psychologists agree.) Men – and women – basically want to kill each other, and the rules of civilization struggle to keep this tendency in check. 'Hence ... [the] commandment to love one's neighbour as oneself – a commandment which is really justified by the fact that nothing else runs so strongly counter to the original nature of man.' Freud says you can get rid of property, abolish monogamous marriage, allow complete freedom of sexual life, but you will still be left with the fact that human beings are fundamentally not nice. Free love is never going to solve the problem.

Our difficulties today have shifted substantially. There was the sexual revolution of the 1960s and 1970s. (And although much of the thinking behind the break with sexual conventions had its roots in psychoanalytic theory, Freud was increasingly slated for being a normative, anti-feminist, nineteenth-century bourgeois. They were clearly too busy having sex to read.) Now, instead of a rigid code of propriety, we are faced with an insistence on constant satisfaction. Everyone is meant to be permanently, perfectly orgasmic. You can have as much sex as you like – and you are even allowed to admit you enjoy it. The most mainstream women's magazines are full of advice about sexual positions, blowjob techniques and the advantages of bisexuality. I'm sure it makes for a better read than recipes and cleaning tips, but it comes with a backlash. Just because you're allowed to do what you like, it doesn't follow that you will actually like it. Having sex with loads of faulty, problematic people can be just as dull and disappointing as getting stuck with one. The only advantage is that you don't stick around long enough to find out how horrible they *really* are. You can feel just as lonely at an orgy as you can on your own at home. The Internet might promise millions of available bodies but that doesn't solve the problem of intimacy (plus they generally seem a bit nicer in the pictures than they do in real life.) The insistence on enjoyment can bring a sense of dissatisfaction. Even when things are going okay, maybe they ought to be going better. You like your partner, but does he/she *really* excite you? Are you fully realizing your dreams? Or should you be expecting more … and more … and more? You may end up sleeping around for the promised bigger thrills but are left feeling emptier than ever.

In his 1974 book *Sexual Behaviour in the 1970s*, Morton Hunt outlines the problem very beautifully:

Relatively few people, even today, manage to make permissive marriage work at all, let alone work better than exclusive marriage. For although marriage no longer has the structural support of religion, community, law, or practical necessity, today there is something else that makes exclusivity, or the appearance of it, immensely important – namely, the loneliness and disconnectedness of modern life, which creates a deep need in modern man and woman to belong, and to have a binding emotional connection to someone else.

While you can now supposedly choose to live however you like, there are new reasons to wish for old-fashioned, exclusive relationships. The alienating speed and chaos of our culture may make us long for something stable, a space in which we can be particular, which gives us the time and safety to know and be known by another person.

There is a theory that says the reason interplanetary contact will probably never take place is that the technology which would make this sort of communication possible is too close to the technology that would destroy a planet. As soon as any species has the means to get in touch … boom! … it's all over. It seems like something vaguely analogous may be happening in the field of romantic love. As soon as it becomes socially acceptable to explore any and all forms of alternative relationship, it suddenly becomes more interesting to stick with one person. But there's still the question of whether monogamy is actually possible – or at least whether it's possible to be happy this way.

There are a number of viable answers. One is that we stop being so clingy and pathetic and learn to have properly intimate non-exclusive relationships. (Although of course this sort of polyamory brings with it a deluge of new and interesting problems, which we'll get onto later.) Another solution appears to be sneakily embedded in Hunt's paragraph. As he rather delicately puts it, 'exclusivity – *or the appearance of it*' (my emphasis) is what a lot of people seem to need. According to this logic, the informed, modern answer is exactly the same as the 'compromised' traditional one. You have to cheat. But you have to do it really well so that your partner doesn't get a whiff of it. (The only difference these days is that men and women are equally licensed in this respect.) It's realistic, relatively honourable and, as long as it all goes to plan, it doesn't do too much harm. For people with children it's probably a lot fairer and better than serial monogamy. There *is* the fact that you're bound to get caught, but you'll just have to deal with that when it happens. With luck, your partner is secretly at it too and will therefore be understanding. The other problem is that, in order for it to work, you have to *pretend* to buy this third solution: real, genetic, sexual and social monogamy. Very discreet cheating is not an ethos you can openly subscribe to. And then there's the fact that maybe this third option may *actually work* – human beings might be freaky enough to be exclusive and like it. The thing about us that marks us out from other creatures is that we seem to be very good at inventing stuff (even if half the stuff we invent isn't actually that good for us). Read any self-help book on monogamy (actually don't, they're all boring) and it will tell you that in order for it to go well you have to be ingenious. You have to talk openly and interestingly. You have to do funny stuff in bed, *and* out of it. You have to work out ways to resolve your conflicts without hating each other too much. In short, you have to be clever as hell. Monogamy, far from being a dreary choice, may be the ultimate arena for romantic and sexual innovation. Like poets who use strictly limiting mathematical forms, painters with a monochrome palette, or novelists who omit the letter E, *serious* monogamists – as opposed to those square *serial* types – may find themselves at the cutting edge of experimental romance. There is a case for *real* monogamy as the greatest human perversion. (And if that fails you'll just have to turn your fertile, visionary brain to thinking up ways to explain where you were between seven and nine last night.)

8.

Things are Swingin'

Are multiple relationships a good idea?

♥ ♥

In which we consider polyamory, swinging and
fuck buddies in our quest for alternatives to
claustrophobic and cloying relationships

———

IT IS BETTER TO BE UNFAITHFUL THAN TO BE FAITHFUL
WITHOUT WANTING TO BE.

Brigitte Bardot

I s it possible to enjoy the pleasures of love without the stifling
gloom? In Kierkegaard's *Diary of a Seducer*, our hero Johannes
tells us: 'I am an aesthete, an eroticist, who has grasped the
nature and the point of love, who believes in love and knows it
from the ground up, and I reserve for myself only the private
opinion that no love affair should last more than a half a year
at most, and that any relationship is over as soon as one has
enjoyed the ultimate.' While lots of people might agree with his
six-month prognosis, they might blanch at his response to it.
Johannes' way out is to cause the object of his desire, Cordelia, to
fall madly in love with him, possibly to sleep with him (it's very
discreetly written), and then for him to ditch her. In this way he

enjoys all the benefits minus the snags. He can experience the fascination and the idealization without the ensuing moany dullness and bad breath in the morning. In his opinion, 'Once resistance is gone, love is only weakness and habit.' The best one can do is to drag out the preliminaries, and then to end it all as soon as it's consummated. This will supposedly be good news for Cordelia too. Dear Johannes is teaching her about eroticism and true love, while saving her from the slavery of marriage. It's all very logically worked out. But is this the best way? Or are there other solutions to the fact that long-term monogamous relationships can be hard on both parties? The glaring problem with Johannes' clever scheme is that it's extremely unkind to Cordelia – although she may of course take the opportunity to become a poet or nun, finding herself much better off in the long run. But surely there must be other methods that don't inflict so much pain.

Some of the most brilliantly logical, and possibly ethical, alternatives are provided by the polyamorists and swingers who don't get stuck in the sticky dyads that so many of us seem to feel are the only available option. Instead they do trios, or even quads – or stick to their primary couple but sleep with other people. Swingers report an unusually high level of marital satisfaction. A 2000 survey conducted by Bellarmine University (a Catholic university in Louisville, Kentucky) found that 79 per cent of swingers described their marriages as 'very happy', compared with 64 per cent of couples in the General Social Survey. But are there new problems that arrive with these solutions? And are these unconventional set-ups really available to everyone, or do you have to be a certain sort of person to enjoy it? (And why do I keep quoting statistics when I don't even believe in them? Sixty-four per cent of conventional marriages are 'very happy'? Yeah, right.)

Frubbly or Wibbly?

Polyamorists are big on neologisms. Not only have they had to invent a new word to describe themselves, they also have words for minor explosions of unexpected jealousy (wibbles) and the enjoyment one can get from seeing one's lover with someone else (it makes you feel so frubbly!). Frubbliness can also be referred to as 'compersion', a word coined by the Kerista community. The Keristans got together in the San Francisco Bay Area in the early 1970s and were big proponents of polyamory. They were much concerned with promoting polyamorous prac-tices, and speaking out against monogamous marriage, amongst other social norms. They published zines and organized weekly 'rap sessions', where visitors and members blasted each other with a harsh DIY form of therapy known as 'gestalt-o-rama'. Sleeping plans were made around Best Friend Identity Clusters – or B-FICs – with the pairings listed on a chore wheel (referred to by the Keristans as 'the washing machine').

No single relationship was given more time than any other. Nobody had their own room. Some of these groups contained as many as eighteen people – nine men and nine women – and were 'polyfidelitous', meaning that members agreed not to sleep with anyone outside the group. They were also heterosexual –

luckily for the people organizing the rotas, or the mathematics might have got a bit complicated. Even Eve (aka Eve Furchgott), a long-time Keristan, writes about the advantages of this sort of set-up: 'The broader ramifications of this family structure are potentially quite significant, because of the problems it solves (loneliness, jealousy, social fragmentation, housing shortages, single parenting, economic strain, emotional boredom) and because of the new vistas of responsible hedonism it opens up.' Not only does it all make emotional sense, it's an economic good bet too. The Keristans were famous for their business acumen, becoming highly successful Mac resellers. They were also admired for having come up with a cannier solution to the AIDS problem than simply getting stuck with one person whose sexual history you knew. Now you could get stuck with seventeen familiar people instead. They aimed to balance a pleasure-seeking lifestyle with strict socialist principles (that nonetheless allowed for the development of a multi-million-dollar business) and, for a while it seems, they succeeded.

Things eventually fell apart for a number of reasons. The founder of the commune, a charismatic beardy called Jud, gradually became more domineering and difficult to be around. And, as the second-hand-computer business took off and people became more involved with the outside world, the Keristans realized there were probably better ways to spend their time than having their lives controlled by some bear with a Jesus complex. But they held it together for twenty years, which is a good deal longer than a lot of marriages, so something must have been working.

♥

These days polyamory is supposedly more widespread than ever. Kerista-style set-ups are still relatively uncommon, but multiple love relations are seemingly thought by lots of people to be a good idea. There are websites and polyamory meet-up groups in most major cities. This networky chatroominess may be because talking seems to be a very important part of the whole enterprise. This is presumably because these people have quite a lot of stuff to work out. When you expand from a couple to a triad or a quad, there are a whole new set of interpersonal issues to deal with. There are thorny issues such as the sharing of sex toys – offer up your own genitals by all means but, please, not the jointly purchased butt plugs. Not to mention finding ways to bolster your primary's 'compersion' (enjoyment) in the face of your new erotic obsession. It can't be easy.

Then there's the knotty issue of scheduling. How often can you see a secondary or tertiary partner? Do you allocate times with your primary – say, once a fortnight? And what if that doesn't line up with their complex poly diary arrangements? How flexible is everyone prepared to be? Some polys talk about using computer spreadsheets to keep things running smoothly. Boundaries, apparently, are everything. Just because you can see other people, that doesn't mean you can mysteriously vanish for the whole weekend and expect to come home to a warm fire and a shepherd's pie. When and where things happen need to be respectfully negotiated. Some couples allow for sleepovers, some don't. Some are prepared to let secondaries into their homes and beds, some aren't. In short, every niggly little detail needs to be worked through openly otherwise you risk ending up in the sorts of mess that regular unfaithful people land themselves in.

Jealousy is a much-discussed poly issue. The interesting thing is that almost no one claims *not* to feel it. It isn't that a poly is a special kind of emotional freak who just happens not to mind the thought of their lover in someone else's bed. Apparently they often mind like mad. But they have developed special ways of thinking about what it means and how to deal with it. On the one hand it means that you too are free to sleep with other people. If this is what you want, then it gives you the incentive to tolerate it when your partner does it too. But, more importantly, jealousy is seen as an emotion that you can learn from. Why should it matter to you that you are the only person who is allowed close contact with your partner's body? Is it because you think you own them? What rights do you imagine your feelings for your partner give you? Does their being involved with someone else *really* take something away from you? Or is it the very thing that will make your long-term relationship possible?

In *The Ethical Slut*, the authors Dossie Easton and Catherine A. Liszt give impeccable advice on everything from what to tell your children about your polyamorous lifestyle to how to behave at a gang-bang. Their line on jealousy is this: 'The way to unlearn jealousy is to be willing to experience it. By actively choosing to experience a painful feeling … you are already starting to reduce its power over you.' The worst thing you can do is to act up, smashing cups and sending forty cranky texts, pretending that your thirst for destruction is somehow someone else's fault. If you feel jealous it's because YOU feel jealous. So the best thing you can do is to sit back and ask yourself what jealousy is. The point with jealousy is to disempower it by submitting it to interrogation. Maybe you are worried that the other person will be better in bed. Or that the backs of their thighs are smoother. Or that they have read more Latin poetry than you. Perhaps you secretly wish you could keep your lover in the cellar so they would never know that there are more attractive, brighter people out there. (Or at least if they did know, there wouldn't be much they could do about it.) But it's your feeling these things that's the problem. You need to sort it out. And, anyhow, if your lover leaves you for someone with smoother thighs, you are probably better off without them.

So polyamorous people are practically saints. Or are they? Is it really that they have devised a far more practicable and realistic approach to relationships? Or do they just get off on a certain sort of pain? Perhaps, like Ava in chapter three, they get an unconscious Oedipal kick out of the idea of their loved ones fucking – just like Mummy and Daddy. Polyamorists often discuss notions like 'the compersion at the heart of jealousy'. Basically, they love it. But in a sense it doesn't matter. If you've found a harmless way to enjoy yourself, then good luck to you. Still, it leaves open the question of whether just anyone can join their ranks. Some see it as a sexual persuasion, much like bisexuality or masochism. You may 'discover' that you are poly-amorous at some point in your life. Or it may be something you have 'always known' about yourself. On the other hand you might be talked into it by a hectoring partner (obviously less harmless). Or you may train yourself into it because it appeals to your sense of good reason. In any case, if you think you can hack the jealousy and the Byzantine timetables, then perhaps polyamory could offer a workable solution to the frustrations and limitations of monogamy.

Swing for Your Supper

Swinging and polyamory are not at all the same thing. While some swingers might be polyamorous, and vice versa, swingers tend to put the emphasis on sex, while polyamorists foreground love. And while swingers don't generally have a bad word to say about their lovey-dovey colleagues in non-monogamy, the polys can be pretty mean about the swingers. Poly websites are full of warnings to those lower life-forms who think it's okay to send in pornographic stories or post pictures of their genitals online. It's clear that these activities have no place in the emotionally verbose world of the multiple lover. Polyamory is about enjoying the intricacy of human emotions, and sex is just a part of that. If you get off on porn, do it in your own time. Swingers, on the other hand, advertise on websites where the only personal information they give is an image of their tits/bum/penis and a list of their preferred sexual practices. Quaint swinger signals like planting pampas grass in the front garden and coyly placing cans of Pledge in the window have been swept aside in favour of more explicit digital displays.

Having said all that, if you approach swingers in the wrong way, you'll find they can be pretty offended by prattlers. For instance, I thought it would be nice to meet some chirpy swingers and talk to them about themselves and their love lives, in the hope that they could teach me something, and that I could pass their wisdom on. To this end I put ads on a few sites inviting experienced swinging couples to speak to me as part of my research for a book. Within less than twenty-four hours I had been banned from their sites. For life! Apparently it's seriously NOT okay to invite swingers to speak. It's a horrible breach of etiquette. And now even if I want to start swinging I won't be able to because I have been marked out as the kind of trouble-maker who might have awkward questions about the appeal of dogging or bukkake. These people are tough. (Don't worry, I'm not really that technologically naïve. I can set up false online identities with the best of them.)

There are plenty of swingers' testimonies out there, however, mainly with titles like 'Our First Time' or 'French Holiday Fun'. These sometimes even claim to tell 'the truth' about what swingers really get up to. They tend to follow a pretty tight format: a person or couple meets some other people or couples and they quickly get down to some group action. It's all really great and everyone ends up perfectly satisfied. They might feel a bit awkward at first but they soon get over it and then it's just 'so horny to see my Gary pumping away at Simona' or whatever. Self-reflection doesn't feature. There's definitely no mention of jealousy, competition or confusion. And no imagination or originality. It was like reading low-grade porn, complete with bad grammar and spelling mistakes, and seemed to confirm every snobbish, preconceived notion about stupid, boring people being stupid and boring together, surrounded by hideous decor. Especially when you are still reeling from your LIFETIME BAN.

The only way to get over this bias, I found, was to read Catherine Millet's *The Sexual Life of Catherine M*. Her grammar is Frenchly elegant. Plus she makes it clear that she wears extremely nice clothes, and that the orgies she attends are peppered with tasteful, modernist furniture. (Unless, of course, she is naked at an outdoor gang-bang in the Bois de Boulogne.) She also writes with a frankness that does away with the nauseating kitschiness of most porn. It's good to hear that, at one very large orgy, she 'chose to fuck only with [her] arse' but can't recall whether this was because she 'was ovulating or had a touch of the clap'. While she feels little need to discuss the subjective effects of submitting her body to hundreds, if not thousands, of encounters, she is great on describing the technical realities. For instance: 'I seem to remember quivering and roaring with laughter between their streams of urine.' It's also interesting to hear that she does actually fall in love and experience jealousy. She repeatedly kicks one of her partners while he's fucking another woman.

The great virtue of her book is that she clearly doesn't feel guilty about any of it – or at least not guilty in a way that would make her stop, or even cause her to publish her book anonymously. Catherine Millet is no Pauline Réage (the pseudonymous author of *The Story of O*) – everyone knows exactly who she is and what she gets up to. This goes against the often-stated idea that most swinging is initiated by manipulative, letchy men, and that their impressionable wives and girlfriends just go along with it for fear of losing them.

Another unusual thing about Catherine Millet is that she is a swinger who clearly likes to articulate herself. While the polys insist on their 'rap sessions', I'd imagine you'd be hard pressed to find a therapy room at a swingers' party. But Millet isn't inclined to ask too many questions about *why* she likes what she likes, she is more interested in documenting it in words. She tells us that she grew up as part of a big family in a small house, and was obsessed with numbers – more particularly with the number of husbands one was allowed to have. But that's about all the background info we get. She also tells us she has never given too much thought to her sexuality, but has simply got on with trying to enjoy herself. It only occurs to her to write a book when, in middle age, she realizes she can have an orgasm perfectly easily with a vibrator, and that she doesn't actually need to have sex with other people. Only then does it become necessary to involve others through the medium of writing.

It seems that swingers are more inclined to satisfy their drives with direct action, while polys are interested in exploring attachment and its various meanings and consequences. Take your pick. As we've hinted before, love consists largely of words.

A Swinger Speaks …

I would have liked to get my hands on a swinging evangelist, but since the ones in the throes of a good time just didn't seem like they were going to talk to me (their energies are directed elsewhere), I will have to offer you an infidel instead. The only swinger I found who was willing to talk was an ex-swinger – and precisely the kind of ex-swinger who has regrets and wonders what the hell she was doing. Although the statistics on swinging present an image of an unusually cheerful group of people, it seems that the best you are going to get out of the happy ones is a quick bit of questionnaire-style box-ticking. If they're prepared to take it further then they probably aren't swingers any more. This is something like Eubulides' liar paradox – if you talk about being a swinger, you can't actually be one. Anyhow, the advantages of this particular candidate were that she was above averagely pleasant and had a very engaging way of speaking. Her story is one of bungalows in the suburbs with overflow car parks and swimming pools smelling of sperm. She spoke about crotchless fishnet suits and dowdy couples with plastic bags full of cock rings and nipple clamps. There was talk of swinging etiquette and long lists of rules. She also mentioned bringing your own drinks and putting your names on the bottles with sticky labels. In short, she didn't make it sound glamorous. She said the problem for her with swinging had always been a voice at the back of her head saying, 'You're not seriously going to do this, are you?' Plus the fact that she never stopped finding it odd that people could simply have sex with each other so matter-of-factly and with so few preliminaries.

As well as swinging parties, she also experimented with meeting other couples online and with having sex in front of a live-broadcast webcam. While some of it was evidently very exciting, there was also an air of tragedy around it. In her own words, 'The thing about swinging is that it can be really dreary, or just fucking sad.' While she had enjoyed fantasizing about it with her boyfriend for two years before actually trying it out, the bare reality seemed less titillating. And when this boyfriend arranged for five strange men to come round in the middle of the night she finally called a halt to the proceedings and bailed out. As she puts it, 'If you can actually believe that it is what it says it is, then fine. You know, "Some people go skiing, some people go swinging." But I don't see how you can just do that stuff and carry on as if everything's normal. If you're an analyser, it can't work. Talking about it is definitely better than doing it.'

While it may appear to be a very practical solution to the limitations of monogamy – you can have loads of sex with other people without cheating on your partner – it might not be the easiest lifestyle to swallow. But had I just stumbled upon one of the unlucky few for whom swinging didn't work out? As with illuminating conversations, reliable statistics on practising swingers are hard to come by. Many of the statistics are collected at swingers' events, where couples are more likely to claim to be having a great time. But swinging gets a mention in about one per cent of divorce cases. And as swingers are thought to make up about one per cent of the population, this doesn't bode well. It's generally understood that swinging doesn't help troubled relationships; it can only work if the couple are very sure of each other's love, and if both members of the couple happen to be the swinging type. All in all it seems that swinging is probably only a good idea for a relatively small number of people, and that it couldn't provide anything like a workable approach for most of us struggling with the conflicting demands of curiosity and fidelity. Perhaps, as our ex-swinger suggests, the best we can get from it is the occasional bit of light relief provided by talking or fantasizing about it.

Friends with Benefits

At the end of the 1960s Serge Gainsbourg and Jane Birkin released their notorious, orgasmic single, '*Je t'aime...moi non plus*' ('I love you ... neither do I'). It was a huge hit all over Europe, despite being banned in five countries and denounced by the Vatican. Casual sex – or 'free love', as it used to be called – had been very much in popular consciousness for a few years. But it seems there was still plenty of guilt around the whole matter. Love and sex had traditionally been tied together, as if it was unthinkable that they could ever be unknotted. Before the 1960s, so the story goes, if you loved someone then you married them and had sex exclusively with them for evermore. (Or you didn't – but at least there was a standard in place which you could either live up to or not.) In the 1960s that idea came very much unstuck. But you can't kill off centuries of dogma without a few death spasms. Gainsbourg's song dealt with the subject of sex without love. Apparently it was common practice at the time to say 'I love you' in bed when you didn't mean it. Everybody knew you didn't mean it – it was just a leftover from the olden days when things like that still mattered. Perhaps it made it possible for relative strangers to jump on each other without feeling too weird about it. The notion of love was still floating around in there somehow, even just as a bit of insignificant noise. The world hadn't changed beyond recognition.

These days we are supposedly much more hardened to the idea that you don't have to be head-over-heels in order to get into bed with someone. Sex is nice – as are eating sweets and playing tennis – and love is very difficult. It makes good pragmatic sense to sleep with people you simply *like*, and not get in a state about making big life choices and giving up certain freedoms. You shouldn't have to lie to each other about what you are doing; it's a perfectly sensible, respectful way to go about life. Casual sex is good; it's a no-brainer. So why does it so often turn sour?

As with every other burning issue in contemporary life, there is a great deal of Internet debate concerning the difference between a friend with benefits and a fuck buddy. Some would say the former implied a more serious friendship, with sex as a non-essential extra, while the latter suggests regular-ish sex without there necessarily having to be much talking or closeness. Friends with benefits (or 'level-two friends') might agree to forgo the sex but keep up the other stuff when a serious lover appears on the scene, while a fuck buddy would probably be expected to recede into the distance. Fuck buddies would be more likely to make a booty call, while a friend with benefits would never be so crass. Other people say there's no difference, it's all just about trying to get the odd bit of sex in a dry period.

Lots of people seem to agree, though, that casual sexual relationships are good in theory, but that they have a habit of turning out more complicated than you might initially have expected. The usual pattern is for one half of the pair to start to have deeper feelings for the other. The more 'in love' half may even have had these feelings from the beginning, but played them down in the hope that the other person could gradually be brought round. To avoid the sorts of upset and accusations that so commonly spring from situations like this, it's thought to be a good idea to lay down certain ground rules from the beginning. But this can be difficult to do when the bottom line is, 'I don't like you *that* much, so don't get any big ideas.' The trick is to find a suitable euphemism. Of course there are plenty of generic ones available, from, 'I'm not really looking for a relationship right now,' to 'I'm still getting over my last relationship,' or even 'You're too good for me – I'd only let you down.' The problem with these (and perhaps with the ones you invent yourself) is that, to a certain sort of person, they function as an aphrodisiac. Remember the Marilyn Monroe character Sugar Kane in *Some Like it Hot*? When Shell Oil tells her he is totally emotionally and sexually cut off, she can't resist trying to cure him. She sees his detachment as a tragedy he needs to get over, plus it provides the perfect arena for her to show how good she is at being a woman. He is perfectly well aware of all this and uses it to seduce her, while making her feel like she is the one taking the initiative. In this way he gets a lot further than he might have if he'd simply jumped on her. By claiming to be unobtainable he gives her something to prove. This is a very likely outcome of telling someone you're currently incapable of love. So what might sound like a plausible ground rule to one person could easily look like a romantic red rag to another.

While the idea of a fuck buddy appears nicely pragmatic, it can be hard to sustain. The amount you like the other person needs to be very precisely gauged; too much and you're risking a romance, too little and you risk being very bored. A bit like the gap between the past and the future, the qualities that make for the perfect fuck buddy occupy an infinitely thin zone. The good thing, though, is that they don't need to be perfect. That's the whole point in them. If it's not working, then you stop it. You don't even need to split up. If you have obeyed the ground rules then you have no duty to the other person. And if you haven't, more fool you. Fuck buddies promise to be the emotional equivalent of a decaffeinated skinny latte. You can get some of the enjoyment, but without the jitters and the voluptuous, creamy taste. But there's always the risk that some scatty barista has mixed your drink with someone else's and, halfway through the cup, you suddenly find that your hands are shaking and there's a sticky sensation in your mouth.

While Shell Oil knew precisely what he was up to with Sugar, lots of us don't have a clue what we really, really want. We might claim to be after something casual, while being secretly pleased that the other person is painfully in love with us. We may be possessive and insistent on monogamy, while entertaining wild fantasies about sex with other people. Perhaps in the field of love and sex more than almost any other, people are very keen to dissemble – to the point of fooling even themselves. The ones who announce that they will never settle down suddenly get hitched. And the ones who say they need space might be the most desperate to consume their love objects. When we display our emotions, we are always at risk of embarrassment and exposure. Having sex may reveal a lot about you, but the way in which you love someone gives away even more.

While sex without love might be considered perfectly normal, it doesn't follow that it's unproblematic. It appears to be difficult for many of us to go through the motions of intimacy without the spectre of proper intimacy being stirred up. So, if love is that difficult to get rid of, it might be best to get back to thinking about how best to deal with it when it rears its grisly head.

Acting Like Grown-ups

Though their methods and rules may vary, polyamorists, swingers, friends with benefits and fuck buddies are all essentially experimenting with different ways of forming non-exclusive attachments to people. And, if we're to take Freud seriously, it seems that they may have grasped a fundamental truth about human relationships that may have eluded those who are still searching for their perfect 'other half' or their 'one true love'. According to Freud, adult relationships are always an attempt to find a more acceptable way to love than the way we did when we were infants. In our first experience of love (for our mother) we were too attached, too clingy and needy. We had to give something up, to stop being babies. People would have told us not to be so stupid, not to cry, not to sulk, not to show off so much (like silly old Gracie). We had to separate from the people we loved, let them get on with other things, stop trying to be the exclusive focus of their attention. Perhaps we were made to feel so ashamed of our obsessive attachments that we went too far the other way; we have persuaded ourselves that we don't need anyone. Perhaps our mothers let us cling to them in order to avoid making choices about their own lives, and now every love object threatens to swamp us just like she did. Perhaps our parents weren't there enough to give us anything to attach to and now we make flaky bonds with whoever's around, like sentimental pieces of dandruff. Perhaps our parents were totally perfect and now we can be happily married just like them. (I've never met one of these but, logically, they need to be taken into consideration.)

In any case, it's almost inevitable that you will be running some kind of emotional dual system, not unlike a computer with Intel Core 2 processing. Only instead of 'increasing your multitasking power with energy efficient performance' you find yourself split in two, wondering which half to take seriously. What are you? An infant who wants to be held and cared for? Or a sensible grown-up who needs space? Or both? But how to be both – *and* do it with another divided person who equally doesn't know what's good for them? Most of us have had to make the shift from a mother/child dyad to a network of multiple loves. We realize (unless we are Norman Bates) that we are better off if we can form bonds with people other than our mums. We persuade ourselves it's a good idea to be part of a broad structure, as opposed to an enclosed unit. And perhaps in adulthood we have the option to choose again between trying to sustain an intense bond with one other person or linking ourselves with a number of others. The interesting thing is that, in psychoanalytic terms, the original dyad has tended to be seen as the archetypal ideal relationship, while the ensuing network is seen as a terrible step down. This is very much in opposition to the free-floating modern idea that married couples are boring but multiple lovers are a riot. Perhaps they're both boring and interesting, but for different reasons. And why *should* you know precisely what's best for you? Maybe it's inevitable that you'll always fantasize about the opposite of what you've got – as will your partner(s).

This is presumably where things like ground rules come in. These ground rules might be anything from the vows that govern a conventional marriage to etiquette-heavy swinging relationships to the fabulous mathematics of the Keristans. They promise to regulate the difficulty of getting involved with another person (or people). In a sense it makes no difference whether you are a swinger or a stay-at-home spouse. Our initial human instinct is to want another person to be ours and ours exclusively for every second of the day, so everyone has to learn to love in a way that doesn't come naturally. Either you do it in the way you think is acceptable, and lose the 'authenticity' of the infantile love you gave up, or you love like a screaming brat and risk losing your self-respect and the respect of the person you're in love with. In short, you have to choose between accepting a loss or limit from the outset, or trying to get *all* of what you want at the risk of turning into a monster. Perhaps the two of you become screaming brats together, which is nice until it becomes apparent that there are no adults around to regulate and you start biting each other's faces and there's never anything to eat in the fridge. Ground rules are like cardboard-cutout policemen. They promise to guide you when your own internal compass is lacking. In other words, they are a nice idea, but extremely easy to kick over.

Testing, Testing ...

It seems that attachment almost invariably triggers difficult feelings in people, whether it's the need to cling tighter or the wish to escape. Any kind of relationship is bound to generate surprises. It's all very well to say that we are modern people and we don't need to construct our sexuality like Victorians, but these new forms of relationship come with as little guarantee of happiness as the old forms. This isn't to say that we should stop experimenting, but maybe that all types of relationship need to be seen as equally experimental – as we saw with Carrie and Big. Getting married could be the weirdest thing in the world to try. It might generate far more interesting results than five simultaneous casual flings. It all depends on how you come at it.

But what would be the distinction between a speculative modern marriage (in which you get to try some interesting things out) and an old-skool property-fest (in which you don't)? Is the difference simply that you can get out of it more easily? Or might it be possible to conceptualize the whole thing another way? One means of doing this would be to acknowledge that people are complex and that rules don't really work. Marriage can never actually be what it promises to be. Nor can swinging. Nor can polyamory. It's not that the various formats actually offer any sort of solution in themselves. Once you've picked one, you'll soon discover its shortcomings. There might be one framework that appeals to you more than the others, but it won't be able to solve the problem of what you are. What you want is likely to exceed what's possible. What you get is always going to be both more and less than you bargained for.

So, if all human interactions are fundamentally impossible to regulate, you're just going to have to be as ingenious as you can be within your limited means. You'll have to invent your relationships as you go, with the help – and hindrance – of the other person or people. You'll have to take them seriously. You'll have to ignore them. You'll have to be careful with them, but not too much. You'll have to try to work out what it takes to make things tolerable. You'll have to build something, and then probably rebuild it, and then carry on making endless adjustments.

Between Buddy Holly's 'Love is Strange', the Eurythmics' 'Love is a Stranger' and Tom Petty's 'Ain't Love Strange' there seems to be some consensus that love is a bit ... well ... strange. And not only is it a weird and exceptional feeling in itself, it can also alert you to the fact that the person you are doing it with is ultimately unknowable. However much you might like to, you can't climb inside their head. Love is an activity that should make you question what a human being is. The closer you get to someone, the more mysterious they might seem. (G.U.R.U! But what on earth R U?) You can go on what they say, or even what they do, but this may be different from what they think, and what they think consciously may be different from what they dream about. They probably don't know who or what they are either. They may have no clue what they're trying to do with you (even if they claim otherwise). And this blurriness of theirs will obviously have some effect on you and your dodgy, divided self too. (Into me I don't exactly see either.) There's really no knowing what you're stumbling into with each other. If love begins with an image and a wish, it generally continues with an unveiling and a shock. But if, unlike Kierkegaard's Johannes, you think you can cope with the exposure of love that lasts beyond six months, then it might be possible to make something unique, if a little wonky. Remember Morton Hunt's observation about the comfort of intimacy within the speed and impersonality of modern life: while you might work all day doing something you hate, then watch other people's lives on TV while being intermittently blasted with adverts for things you don't want, your love life could be the one place you can construct something of your own. Of course it will be done in collaboration with other people and will therefore never be *exactly* what you want. But, if you work with other experimenters, you will invariably generate awkward revelations, charming oddities and unexpected collisions. As with any art, you needn't work in a strange medium in order to produce something new. Whether you are a married couple or a quad or an eighteen-person B-FIC, you might be best off giving up any hope that there can be any broadly applicable guidelines and simply launch yourself delicately into the mess. And where Kierkegaard's Johannes saw 'weakness and habit', you may even be clever enough to conjure up curiosity and strength.

9.

Boys and Girls

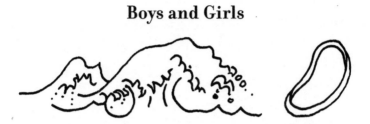

Do men and women behave differently in love?

♥ ♥

In which popular dating manuals are read in the light of queer theory and neuroscience – and we are forced to realize that nothing about gender makes any sense

THERE IS MORE DIFFERENCE WITHIN THE SEXES
THAN BETWEEN THEM.

Ivy Compton-Burnett

I t's not unusual for a straight man to wonder once in a while whether or not another man might understand his emotional and sexual needs better than a woman does. And plenty of gay men complain about how much they despise gay culture, longing for the supposed 'normality' of heterosexual life. And for all those women who claim to wish they were lesbians on the grounds that 'women are so much nicer and better than men', there will be a lesbian who will tell you about an ex-lover who slashed her tyres, smashed up her garden and gave her two black eyes. Lesbian domestic violence is not uncommon. A recent survey by Sigma found that 22 per cent of lesbians in the UK reported having been in an abusive relationship, as did 29 per cent of gay men. This isn't so out of sync with Amnesty's claim that one in four women will be a victim of domestic violence in their lifetime. Being gay or straight makes very little difference to the likelihood of your being mistreated in a relationship. It seems that there is no sexual identity that can save you from the devilment that is a relationship. Even celibate people have to deal with their own dreadful selves. But are there nonetheless significant differences in the ways men and women go about love? And, if so, what is the nature of these distinctions? Are they biological? Culturally determined? Or just unfortunate phenomena that can only be explained using interplanetary metaphors?

Heterosexual relationship guides often seem to take it as read that men are men and women are women. There are nice guys and bastards, babes and bunny boilers, but these distinctions are secondary; genital type is the main clue you need when trying to solve the puzzle of who the other person is and what they want from you. To loosely summarize: women want to be desired and listened to by someone they see as strong, while men want to be admired, trusted and left to their own devices by someone they find sexy. These ends can sometimes seem mutually exclusive – she wants to talk about her feelings, he wants to tinker in the shed. So men and women must learn to compromise: shed now, chat later. It's beautiful.

Books about pre-relationship dating generally take a slightly different tack. Both men and women apparently respond well to a lack of interest, but for subtly divergent reasons. Men have to be left alone or they will think you are desperate to marry/incarcerate/physically engulf them, and women are seduced by men who don't appear weak and needy. All men apparently have a built-in cling-on detector, while women have what dating guru David Deangelo rather excellently calls a 'wuss-dar'. So the basic trick is to ignore the people you fancy, but just the right amount.

Lesbian and gay dating advice tends to be slightly less paranoiac. The other person isn't necessarily an alien entity whose strange laws and customs need explanation or they will kill you. Nor are they a separatist state on fierce guard against invaders. Emphasis is more on the pragmatics of dating – mini golf is great for a lesbian first date, apparently, but it's important once things get going to maintain a good level of personal hygiene. Gay men need to learn when to be active and when to be passive in order not to step on each other's toes. According to American TV matchmaker Patti Stanger, the important thing for gay men to bear in mind when looking for love is to 'put your pickle back in your pants'. She tells us it's better to hold off and 'save it for dessert'. But who eats pickles for dessert? For both lesbians and gay men the guidelines say it's important to define 'dating goals' early on as you can't automatically assume – as all heterosexuals do, naturally – that the aim is marriage and children.

The overall fact is that large areas of bookshops and huge swathes of cyberspace are taken up with millions of words aimed at limiting the destructiveness of one's love objects. Whether we are gay or straight we supposedly need to be taught where to take them, what to do with them when we get there, and how soon to call them after we leave. Then we need to know how to continue to relate to them – and finally how to dump them without them demolishing too many of our possessions. The rules of dating are a series of desperate rituals whose aim is to placate what's known in Continental philosophy as the Big Other. We don't really know exactly who or what it is, but if we do or say the right things to it, then there's a hope that it won't rip us to shreds.

So is there really anything sensible to be said about 'what men do' and 'what women want'? Or is the problem more that no one can ever *really* know who anyone else is – male or female – nor decipher what they might be trying to do with us?

Spot the Difference

In *Men are from Mars, Women are from Venus* John Gray appears to be quite confident on the subject of what a man is and what a woman is. It appears to him to be self-evident; a man is a highly pragmatic person with a penis, and a woman is a chatty person with a vagina. Both have very particular ways of going about things which, if incorrectly interpreted, can lead to trouble. 'Martians' stride around making autocratic decisions while 'Venusians' sit around debating the pros and cons of a second cup of tea. If you try to stop a man doing his thing he will feel like you are a leechy harridan out to ruin his life. And if you try to stop a woman talking excessively she will think you are an autistic jerk – plus she may cry. Men and women just have to learn to respect each other's different ways of doing things and they will soon find out that they can make a great team. He can make a tent out of two old tea towels and a lollipop stick and she can add some feminine touches to turn it into a 'home'. He can get the big stuff done and she can make life pleasanter while he does it. Like any mixed-race couple, they can learn to be sensitive to one another's cultures and to create a harmonious, tolerant environment in which love can flourish.

If the Mars/Venus concept isn't enough to get the point across, there are other key metaphors. For instance, when a man is up-set, 'he becomes very quiet and goes to his private cave … When he has found a solution he feels much better and comes out of his cave.' Handy stuff. Or, 'Men are like rubber bands. When they pull away they can stretch only so far before they come springing back.' Ouch! 'A woman is like a wave. When she feels loved her self-esteem rises and falls in a wave motion.' How a reclusive piece of stationery and a volatile liquid are meant to get together and live in suburban bliss is a mystery, but I'm sure André Breton would have found it as 'beautiful as the chance encounter of a sewing machine and an umbrella on an operating table'.

Since it appeared in 1992, Gray's book has sold over forty million copies, and probably been parodied and insulted almost as many times. In 1996, feminist blogger Susan Hamson set up a website, *The Rebuttal from Uranus*, solely devoted to attacking what she sees as Gray's hopelessly sexist views. The problem, as she understands it, isn't simply that he actually believes that men and women can be divided into two neat camps, but that being a good Venusian mainly involves learning to tiptoe around a self-deluding pig.

♥

Shortly before Gray's book came out, the American feminist Judith Butler published *Gender Trouble*. It took ideas from psychoanalysis (particularly the French camp), feminist theory and sociology in order to argue that gender was an artificial construct. Her book sold roughly 39,900,000 fewer copies than *Men are from Mars, Women are from Venus* but, in academic circles, this still makes it a huge bestseller. It proposed that there is nothing natural, or 'essential', about gender. Being a gendered person involves a type of performance; you act like a 'man' or a 'woman' according to a set of rules that pre-exist you. The conventions of these performances have been repeated and honed over the centuries, so much so that people imagine they are somehow inevitable and 'real'. Society coerces you into playing one or the other. Messing with gender roles can land you in all sorts of trouble – which is why, according to a certain logic, *not* playing along might be very radical and worthwhile. A woman with a moustache can be a threat to gendered life as we know it. Or at least this is what certain readers of Butler's book chose to imagine. In the 1990s, while the aliens got on with breeding and bridging the cosmic divide, another group of people got busy applying lipstick, strapping on dildos and hoping that patriarchy would unravel. (And some of us were so stupidly post-modern we even tried to do both.)

Butler's book was largely ignored by the kind of readers who like John Gray, and adored by people who like John Waters (the cult American film director who made the original *Hairspray*, starring Divine, with his undisguised gruff voice and lurid crimplene dresses). But it was also criticized by some of the

French psychoanalytic thinkers whose theories it drew on. It seemed to them too easy to say that gender was simply a performance, albeit one backed up by a millennia-long brainwashing programme. Could you *really* simply decide to play it another way, risking only social disapproval? Or was there something more intractable about it than that? (To be fair, Butler's book acknowledges this problem, but perhaps it gets eclipsed by her central argument which, loosely speaking, is that gender is something you *do* and which, by implication, might therefore be done differently.)

These French thinkers didn't have much time for any simplistic ideas of biology either, so how did they explain this thing that made sexual difference so impossible to unpick? The answer already put forward by Jacques Lacan in 1973 was that one's gender is determined by one's relation to 'the phallus' – and that the phallus isn't simply a piece of meat (ergo, no flambéing) but a highly privileged 'signifier', or symbol. This relationship can be one of either 'having' or 'not having'; men have the symbolic phallus, and women don't – or, to be more precise, men are 'not without having it'. The penis is fallible and fleshy and worryingly detachable, while the phallus isn't an object but an idea. It's a signifier with no signified – a word without a corresponding thing – which means that a biological 'woman' might just as well have it as a biological 'man'. Basically, you can't ever tell just by looking whether you are dealing with a man or a woman – even if the person is naked. It may not even be something you can identify with any certainty about yourself. But, Lacan's argument went, everyone exists in *some* relation to this signifier and will therefore be unable to escape gender (or 'sexuation', as it came to be called). Even if you are born a hermaphrodite, or have operations to give yourself the char-acteristics of both sexes, the law will still require you to register as one or the other. People will insist on your being a 'he' or a 'she' rather than an 'it' – you will always be 'a man with breasts', or 'the girl whose balls dropped'. Language apparently doesn't leave space for indecision.

By this count, biology can't dictate sexual position, though it may nonetheless have some bearing on it. Having a vagina or a penis may hold some sway over which way things go – it's not completely irrelevant – it just isn't the deciding factor. It's up there with other considerations, like whether your parents wanted a boy or a girl, which of them wears the trousers, and which family member you most resemble. Combine that with societal pressure to go one way or the other (preferably in accord with your anatomy, though not necessarily) and you're not exactly left with a tasty menu of mouthwatering intersexual possibilities.

If skimming through Judith Butler leads you to imagine that you might emerge in adulthood with some say in the matter, a closer reading might leave you with the idea that your gender has been very much foisted on you by a vicious combination of language, cultural stereotypes, a construct we call biology, law and very particular events in your life, and that you just have to make the best of it. It's pleasant enough to believe that there might be something you can do to soften the blow, but the notion of a brutal division isn't going to suddenly dissolve. It is impossible to think (or act) your way out of the idea of men and women, no matter how ludicrous and unbearable it is. You might not be able to tell which is which – indeed, there may be no one who is properly either one or the other – but the flawed and failing concept of sexual distinction is irreducible. As Butler puts it, 'what is left is the question of how to acknowledge and "do" the construction [of sexuality] one is invariably in'. It's not much to play with, but it's something.

It's easy to see why writers like John Gray should be so much more popular. He offers a comforting fairy tale about boys and girls; in the blue corner you have the elastic bands, in the pink corner the waves. All you have to do is learn the codes of the opposite sex and they will cease to be a frustrating mystery. While Jacques Lacan managed to perplex and irritate people with notorious statements like 'there is no sexual relation' and 'the woman doesn't exist', John Gray promises to calm everyone down by telling them precisely what men and women are – and claiming that they are perfectly designed to fit together. But while Lacan's proclamations may initially appear counter-intuitive, they seem to be borne out by experience more than the soothing fictions of Gray. There is always something that doesn't quite add up about sexual relationships, and there is no universally applicable definition of femininity or masculinity. You might have the odd nice moment when something seems to make sense, but it'll all screw up again five minutes later.

Still, in the end you have to concede that both Butler and Gray have a point. While it may be the case that gender is a very puzzling matter, it's also true that human beings sometimes do behave according to type. While *Men are from Mars, Women are from Venus* is probably one of the most annoying texts in human history, it would be dishonest to say that it didn't bear any relation to life as it's lived. Forty million readers can't be wrong. In a sense it's not just about whether a man is a man because he's been tricked into thinking he is one, or because God made him that way – while he's retiring to his cave and extending away from his oceanically turbulent missus then she's still going to have to cope with it somehow. It has to be admitted that men sometimes really do behave like 'men', and women have, on occasion, been known to behave like 'women'. You just can't rely on them to do so at all times.

While the archetypes put forward by Gray certainly seem to carry some weight, you can always find counter-examples. A Barbara Cartland can always be offset by a Patricia Cornwell or a Catherine Millet, and a Norman Mailer or a Henry Miller can be played off against a Stendhal. Even Gray himself acknowledges the blurriness of gender. In the introduction to his book, he mentions those couples who've got it all the wrong way round; the man is clearly from Venus and the woman is a Martian. This, he explains, is generally because the man has been sucked into identifying with women and forswearing his true masculinity, while the woman has had to become masculine in order to hold down a job. In his enlightened way he suggests that by applying the techniques in his book these unfortunate couples might not only be able to spice up their relationship, but also to sort out their unfortunate confusion. The man can get twangier, the woman wetter, and both will be happier. Still, it's nice to see that there's a side of John Gray that's every bit as malleable as any queer theorist. While Judith Butler concedes that gender is something you're stuck with, John Gray actually thinks you can change it as you wish.

Game Theory

One of the first really striking dating books of the new millennium was Neil Strauss's *The Game*. It fearlessly buys into the idea of men versus women, turning sexual relations into a fierce battle of wills. Like Gray, Strauss doesn't let himself get bogged down by complex theories of gender. He just steams in like it's all already been decided. In the book, Strauss transforms himself from an AFC (average frustrated chump) into a world-class PUA (pick-up artist). He takes lessons and advice from other PUAs and learns how to neg (flirtatiously insult) and sarge (domineeringly chat up) women. He backs this up with an understanding of how to annihilate an AMOG – the alpha male of a group – with a vital skill known as 'amogging' (making them look stupid). All this is combined with a handful of neuro-linguistic programming tricks and some cod-psychology tests. The amazing thing is that the techniques actually appear to work. By the middle of the book our previously hapless narrator tells us he has eight regular fuck buddies and a drawer full of phone numbers.

Apparently the PUA community wasn't exactly delighted by the book's success. Their secrets were out. Now, if a man goes up to a woman in a bar and asks whether she made her dress out of a pair of old curtains, she may realize that she is simply being 'negged' and that he does in fact fancy her. She will therefore be far less eager to win his approval, knowing that she actually has it already. The power will be on her side and she will do her best to mess with his head. So the central tenet of PUA doctrine – make women feel crap so they're grateful to you for liking them – comes unstuck.

The strength of the book seems to be that it shamelessly refuses to pay lip service to feminism and has no truck with the cheesy, stay-married-for-ever ideals of John Gray. Women are portrayed as desirable, scary and frustrating. Of course you want to sleep with them, but either they don't want to sleep with you at all, or they want to trap you in a dreary relationship. In either case it's annoying. 'The game' is a set of procedures for bypassing women's better judgement and extracting what you want from them. For a woman, this makes for much better reading than endless claptrap along the lines of: 'Just as men can support women by making little changes, women need to do the same.' Thanks for the profundities, John. How much more refreshing to come across passages like, '"We're going to reframe you so you're not glad to have some boopsie sucking your dick," Steve explained. "It will be a privilege for her to drink from the nectar of the master."' It's disturbing and distasteful, but at least you get the sense that Strauss is trying to be honest. As he says at the very beginning of the book, 'Don't hate the player … hate the game.'

The thesis of *The Game* is that there's a war on out there, and the sooner everyone recognizes it the better. If you can develop a working understanding of enemy strategy, good for you. The problem that Neil Strauss finally stumbles across as he hones his battle skills is that knowing how to get women into bed doesn't actually solve your romantic problems. There may eventually come a woman whom you like more than all the others. And she may prove impervious to all your pyrotechnics. She might even think you're a bit of a wanker. This will make you like her more – at last there's someone who can see through your schtick. You drop your artillery in the hope that you can bring her round. You show her more flaky aspects of yourself; you do what you can to prove that your desire for her is unique and authentic – that she's not just another muff on legs. In other words, you're back to square one and no acronyms will save you. You're going to have to invent your own game.

Neil Strauss deals with the breakdown of his tactics with good grace. He realizes that underhand hypnotic techniques and amogging have their limits, that there may be greater satisfactions than tricking naïve women into sleeping with you. He does rather smugly end the book with himself in a happy relationship with Lisa Leveridge, the guitarist from Courtney Love's band. But it's worth it for the pleasure it must have given the people he'd bedded and abandoned to read that she'd dumped him for Robbie Williams not long after publication. Being a world-class PUA can't save you from humiliation at the hands of the opposite sex.

Still, not only do you have to love Neil Strauss for giving away all his secrets, you also have to concede that, in terms of women's empowerment, his book has got to be up there with Marilyn French's *The Women's Room*. What could be more empowering to a woman than the knowledge that men are so scared of her they will go to any length to rob her of just a bit of her terrifying feminine might? And, unlike John Gray, Strauss is very upfront about the limits of the measures he proposes. Not only do the rules break down as soon as you meet someone clever, but they rely on not too many people knowing them. There are very funny moments in the book when it turns out that hundreds of men in LA are using Strauss's methods, thanks to the seminars he and his fellow PUAs have been conducting. You can't go to a nightclub without someone 'doing the cube' on you. (I've not been able to work out exactly what 'the cube' is, beyond it being a pre-rehearsed chat-up technique.) The women of LA knew something was up. As soon as the game goes public, it's over.

Strauss's game is a very conscious performance that involves acting like a man, and hoping that women will react like women. In it, the man has to appear to lack nothing – he has friends waiting for him and, sorry, but he has to go. He's brilliantly cool and well dressed. And he might even be into other men (or at least he doesn't care if you think so). In short, there's nothing he needs from the woman he's sarging. The fact that so much of it relies on presenting an appearance of non-neediness (thereby evading the wuss-dar) is what gives the game away. The player is desperate, but knows how to dissimulate. It's a fairly unsubtle way of advertising that you don't need your mum any more. And also perhaps of announcing that you have the phallus while the other person doesn't. The point is to make your opponent (aka your object of desire) feel that they lack something in order to raise your own value. The fact that men have traditionally done this to women over the centuries is delicately overlooked, perhaps because, as everybody knows, they've only *ever* been doing it because they feel weak and silly. And anyhow women do it to men too, and men do it to men, and women do it to women and, frankly, it must be about time to ask the scientists whether they have anything sensible to say on the subject.

Bio-logic

The idea that gender is a slippery business is hardly new. Being asked to tick 'M' or 'F' should never be considered a simple matter. Scientific studies of sexual difference have tended to use different methods at different times. The Greeks had some rather fanciful theories concerning anatomy. Hippocrates believed that the womb (the 'hyster' in Greek) was an organ that could wander around the body, causing problems as it came into contact with other organs. In the seventeenth century the word 'hysterical' entered the English language when medics came up with the notion that the empty womb filled up with noxious gases, which then rose to a woman's head, making her miserable and hard to get along with. This theory was presumably very useful in legitimizing the idea that women were fundamentally flaky and problematic, whereas men were basically quite functional. In the nineteenth century, despite putting in question some of the most fundamental ideas human beings had about themselves, Darwin continued to believe quite uncritically that women were intellectually inferior to men. He didn't feel a great need to justify himself empirically. But contemporaneous attempts to explain gender differences were centred around the autopsy table. The fact that men's brains were 11–12 per cent heavier was taken as conclusive proof that women were more stupid. In the twentieth century, the emphasis shifted towards IQ tests. The problem here was that different tests produced different results. Sometimes women came out cleverer – it just depended on what you asked them.

Today's scientific theories of sexual difference are no more final or persuasive. It's known that men's brains contain more grey matter related to intelligence and that women's contain more white matter related to intelligence – but neither of these properties actually makes you smarter. Men and women appear to fare equally well at solving mathematical problems. They also appear to be similarly good with language. It doesn't seem to be the case that one lot are good at one thing and that another lot are good at another. Of course there are fewer female mathematicians in history but, as the current scientific position suggests, this seems to have more to do with cultural conditions than natural ability. One theory is that very minor biological differences have been amplified over time, but that these can easily be switched back due to the brain's neuroplasticity. In other words, brains change according to what you do with them; it's easy enough to make a whole bunch of people appear dumb simply by failing to educate them and by not giving them anything interesting to do. And then it's just as easy to flick straight back again. The human brain is anything but hardwired – as can be seen in the cases of victims of head injuries, who can be taught to use different parts of their brains to perform the functions affected by their accidents. It's possible to cultivate the brain in all sorts of different directions. So it's not so strange that people can be persuaded to conform to type. And it's also not so strange that types come a bit unravelled as soon as you stop trying so hard to police them. If we're living through a period where there's slightly less pressure than usual for men and women to act like 'men' and 'women', then it should come as no surprise that we don't. Still, as we've said, that doesn't mean we can simply do what we like. A woman who cultivates leg hair and studies astrophysics may find herself the object of puzzlement or even ridicule. The only difference is that she now has discrimination laws on her side if anyone tries to stand in her way.

But is it just lazy to say that there's nothing to be said about men and women? Isn't there a new and fascinating bit of research in the papers on the subject almost every day? Neuroscientists have worked out why women buy so many shoes! Scientists have discovered why men read in the toilet! Researchers have identified the gene that causes women to worry about the size of their bottoms! The problem when you look closer is that the results are never actually very striking and that you can almost always find some research that tells you exactly the opposite. For instance, it's become popular dogma to claim that there is some neuroscientific back-up for the idea that women are better communicators, while men are better at processing information. This is because grey matter is as-sociated with information processing, while white matter is important in making connections between things. But while it might look as though biology is backing up a cultural stereotype and telling us it was always meant to be that way, it turns out not to be so. In the lab, men and women actually performed equally in both areas. As Richard J. Haier at the University of California puts it, 'Here you have men and women, equivalent in intelligence, with apparently two completely different brain architectures.' There is a difference, but it's still scientifically impossible to give that difference a value.

Perhaps some of the most pernicious 'scientifically' backed up myths have been provided by the evolutionary theorists, whose ideas have been taken up by popular writers and twisted into all sorts of peculiar shapes. For instance, in answer to a letter from a man concerned about his wife's lack of orgasms, a newspaper agony uncle blithely puts forward his thesis that women's orgasms are meant to be less frequent than men's because this encourages them to have more sex. This is argued on the grounds that irregular rewards were proven to be more effective in the training of cats. So irregular female orgasms are therefore surely better for the survival of the species. The agony uncle then tells the author of the letter not to worry about the fact that his wife isn't having such a great time in bed – this is simply what nature intended. This is a speculative theory, entirely made up by a journalist with a short deadline.

If you use evolutionary theory you can usually find a way to argue that men and women are like that for good reason. Men need to hunt so that women can breastfeed. Women talk more because they spend more time at home with children, while men are out running through the forest. So women's brains are built for chit-chat while men's are designed for problem-solving. This is why women are annoying and rabbit on. Or this is why men are robot-like idiots. But when you start to perform tests and experiments it all breaks down. No one knows yet what the differences between men's and women's bodies and brains mean in terms of what we can or should do with them, now or in the future. As soon as you stop believing in the 'naturalness' of sexual difference it all comes unstuck. In science as well as in cultural studies it seems that gender is very much in crisis.

Call Waiting

One of the commonest anxieties of modern dating springs from the question of when it's appropriate to communicate with the other person. Is it nice and spontaneous to email them as soon as you get home from your first date? Or will they think you are a desperate loser? Is it important to make people wait to hear from you? Will this increase their desire? Or will they just think you don't like them? And does it matter whether the man or the woman gets in touch first? Hours of time seem to be passed either in therapy or in the pub with friends worrying over the implications of when to call, with both men and women tying themselves in knots over the various options. Members of both sexes often seem to have some notion about what the other lot are up to. Myths abound: men don't call because they forget about you when you're not there. Women don't call back because they're playing hard to get. Women will be put off if you contact them too soon. Men don't like to be chased.

Problems seem to grow out of the fact that it's not possible to know about who the other person is or what they expect. Double-guessing is the order of the day. In this space where nothing is knowable – your love object is absent and you don't have a clue what they're thinking – it can be tempting to inject your own ideas. But in order for them not to seem like your own ideas it may help to build them out of a pre-existing template. And the template of standard 'male' and 'female' behaviour is one of the easiest to get your hands on. Books like Ellen Fein and Sherry Schneider's *The Rules* attempt to give generic guidelines that can be applied to any dating situation. All men, according to them, are 'thrillseekers' who enjoy a good chase. So all women should play hard to get – and *never* call first or go Dutch on a date. (And Neil Strauss's *The Game* tries to teach men how to give those rigid 'rules girls' a run for their money. Fair play to him.) If you think you know what a man/woman is, then you can fool yourself into imagining you know something about the person whose call you're waiting for. But you don't. You can tell yourself that if she hasn't called back by Wednesday she doesn't like you. Or that you mustn't call him because he needs space. But it's all just a construct to help you deal with the fact that the other person is a total enigma. You can try to tame the Big Other by turning it into a This or a That, but it won't have any effect on *it* – all it can do is to make you feel temporarily less crazy.

Gay people fret equally over when to call or text, but without all the claptrap about gender. Instead they have to come up with their own claptrap about the other person – that super-attractive guys are too arrogant to reply, that she said something about being forgetful when it came to phone-charging, that iPhones don't work properly abroad. Anything you can come up with about another stranger is likely to be a load of rubbish, it's just important to fill those blanks with something.

It seems the problem isn't so much between men and women, but between human and human. Misunderstandings are a fundamental part of relationships. Men can utterly fail to comprehend one another. Women can drive each other round the bend. While Simone de Beauvoir was very wisely pointing out that 'One is not born a woman, one becomes one', her partner Jean-Paul Sartre was equally wisely noting that 'Hell is other people.' It's not about gender – it's worse than that.

10.

Hey, That's No Way to Say Goodbye

Breaking up is hard to do

♥ ♥

In which we try to cobble together a happy ending
out of a whole load of sad ones

I LOVE TO SHOP AFTER A BAD RELATIONSHIP.
I DON'T KNOW. I BUY A NEW OUTFIT AND IT MAKES
ME FEEL BETTER. IT JUST DOES. SOMETIMES I
SEE A REALLY GREAT OUTFIT, I'LL BREAK UP WITH
SOMEONE ON PURPOSE.

Rita Rudner

Love always ends. Sometimes one or both of the lovers die. Sometimes they just go off each other. Sometimes one leaves while the other is still madly in love with them. In any case it's always a bit sad. But it's also a bit happy because it gives them a chance to try again.

All of the above options have their ups and downs. Dying is good because it removes the element of choice (except in the case of suicide and murder). It's bad because it's devastating and irreversible. Mutual disillusionment is at least democratic, if a little depressing. Leaving and being left are revolting, but sometimes also very interesting. Reconstructing yourself after being dumped is an excellent process, a bit like moving house.

(And, if you live together, it sometimes even necessitates moving house so you can really wallow in the metaphor.) Leaving someone who loves you is terrible because it makes you feel like a scumbag. On the bright side, you got away from them, which is presumably what you wanted.

So, the happiest thing about endings is that they are also very often beginnings: a new life, a new love, a new outfit. But how do you know when something's really over? What's the difference between a commitment-phobic quitter and a sensible self-preservationist? Or a hopeless masochist and a romantic idealist? If love is a complicated experiment and can't guarantee happiness, then how can you tell when enough's enough? Do you really need to change the person, or just change your expectations? If death's going to put a halt to the whole thing anyway, then why bother to do it yourself? What if the next beginning is just the start of another end? Is there any point in stopping, or starting? Or are our love lives just a meaningless arrangement of stops and starts? Wouldn't it perhaps be cleverer just to start something and not stop? Or stop the whole business and start something else?

Let's consider the options.

Finishing School

The amazing thing about being left is that it's sublimely out of your control. The other person has made a decision that radically affects your existence and there is nothing you can do about it. You might have helped things along by acting moody in the evenings, being clingy or having an affair, but maybe you just wanted to upset them, not drive them away altogether. Perhaps you've been supremely nice and they are behaving irrationally. Still, it's out of your hands. If they want to leave and you don't want them to, you just have to swallow the pain. Being walked out on can be extremely shocking. It's not so strange to cry for a fortnight, get ill, take time off work, stop eating.

If managing the disappearances and reappearances of another person is central to the project of love, then if someone decides to disappear more permanently it can reactivate all kinds of horrors. The abandoned person is hurled into a terrifying space where they may feel completely incapable of life alone. They become temporarily unable to make their bed, wash their clothes, or pay the gas bill. Consciously, they may tell themselves that this is because all these things seem pathetically unimportant in the face of the fact that their loved one is gone. But perhaps they are regressing to a former state of helplessness. And, like before, they may find themselves trying desperately to work out ways to bring about a reappearance. They try to be everything they imagine the missing person might like. Perhaps they start doing all the things they were accused of not doing before – romantic gestures, love letters, listening. Or they stop doing the annoying things – drinking, taking drugs, criticizing. Perhaps, if they are famous, they appear in public in an extremely nice dress in the hope that the press will print pictures. If they are not famous they just have to hope that a friend will pass on information about how happy/busy/slim they are. This is the grown-up equivalent of not crying when your parents leave you with the babysitter. You are desperately showing your errant love object that you are worthy of their affection. You want them to see that you are a *good thing* because being left can make you feel like a very *bad thing*. It's not uncommon for abandoned people to claim to feel 'like shit'. They identify with what's disgusting and useless. Perhaps they even feel that they have been treated 'like shit', that the abandoner sees them as something unpleasant that needs to be flushed away. The double meaning of the word 'dump' is clearly no coincidence. It becomes crucial to prove to oneself and the world that one is anything but a piece of excrement. Hence the importance of good clothes.

Like any kind of mourning, recovering from being ditched takes a massive psychological effort. You have to attempt to transform yourself from human detritus to desirable object. The loss of your loved one isn't simply a loss of *them*, but also of an image of yourself. Presumably the fact that they used to like you was something you enjoyed. It gave you a sense of self-worth, made you feel like you were someone. They provided the proof that you were loveable. This may even have surprised you. Perhaps you didn't think you were so great. And now here they are telling you that, actually, you were right and they made a mistake. You're not the loveable thing they thought you were – and that you were temporarily prepared to believe in, as if their seeing it in you actually meant it was there. Their adoring gaze is gone and you are back to being the flawed, flailing entity you hoped you'd stopped being. You are returned to the existence you imagined their love might save you from. Your dress is in rags and your car is a pumpkin. In this state you have a number of options (some of which can be usefully combined):

* PROJECTION. You can say that it's not you that's rubbish, it's them. They aren't capable of relating properly. They've barely treated you like a human being. They're sick. They have undiagnosed Asperger's syndrome.

* INTROJECTION. You incorporate some of their qualities in order not to miss them so much. You dress like them, speak like them, eat all their favourite foods. In short, you become them.

* KILLING YOURSELF. They're right, you *are* shit. So don't hang around stinking the place up. (No! I didn't mean it! Of course, you're lovely!)

* KILLING THE OTHER PERSON. How dare they continue to exist when they clearly have such a poor view of you? They are dangerous. They must go. (Not recommended either.)

* AUTO-CRITIQUING. You blame yourself for all the stupid things you did. You see yourself from the other person's point of view and find yourself lacking. You promise yourself that, in future, you'll never make those stupid mistakes again.

* EGO-PUFFING. You tell yourself that you're brilliant and it's their fault if they can't see it. Perhaps you even manage to persuade someone else to fall in love with you very quickly. Or perhaps your own narcissism is up to doing the job all by itself. Lucky you. (Are you just *like that* or did you eat some self-help manuals?)

* ZEN ACCEPTANCE. They are them, you are you. It didn't work out. It's nobody's fault, that's just the way of things. (You are a genius! I love you! But didn't you secretly have to hate yourself and them just a *little* bit first?)

It wouldn't be so strange to contemplate a bit of each. Except the third and fourth ones, all of these phases might be stepping stones on the way to a more bearable state of existence. (And perhaps the person who left you was also some kind of stepping stone to get you over a pre-existing pain.) Each set of ideas constitutes a part of the reconstruction effort as you go about trying to reassemble your junk. If love was something you built in the hope that it might make your life better, now you have to lay down the groundwork for the creation of a new relationship – which may even require a period of trying to be in love with yourself. You just have to piece together whatever mental scaffolding promises to provide relief until you hit on something relatively stable – at which point you will probably find yourself solid enough to meet someone else and the whole process will begin again. Only perhaps it'll be you that walks this time. In which case …

Being the leaver is generally thought to be preferable to being the left. Things are going your way. (This, of course, doesn't apply to cases where you are leaving someone you love but who insults you or hits you, or who lies to you all the time. If this is your story, then stick to the list above.) However, it can still be very upsetting. The other person is likely to want to know why you are doing it. You may or may not be able to tell them. Or at least you will probably only be able to tell them a part of it. Whatever you say is liable to seem unreasonable. As soon as you articulate it, they offer to change it. Or they tell you that it's not really like that. And maybe they're right.

Is any reason good enough for leaving someone you once loved who still loves you? Or is it invariably an unfair and horrible thing to do? There is always the idea that if you just slowed down and thought about it, there'd be a way to work it out. You could do counselling together, or go on holiday. But if you take this logic seriously then you may be stuck with this person for the rest of your life. Of course, if you accept that love is always flawed and difficult, this might not be such a bad fate. If you can't work it out with them, why should you be able to work it out with *anyone*? Perhaps you really would be better hanging about and making a go of it. But then again perhaps you wouldn't. As you can't possibly know which option will produce better results, you're just going to have to go on gut instinct. And if your guts are seriously telling you to get out then you will probably only get stomach cancer if you don't listen.

But this leaves you with the problem of what to say. Do you simply state that if you stay you will probably die soon anyway? That the relationship is killing you? Or do you attempt to be kinder and more constructive? You might try to explain that it's you that has the problem, not them. (But obviously don't *ever* actually say, 'It's not you, it's me,' however tired and frustrated you are.) Their answer to this may be that they like you and your problems and would be happy to put up with them a bit longer. At this point you may have to say, 'You deserve better.' This is the verbal equivalent of just going to the shop to buy some milk and never coming back. There's not much the other person can do about it. They can cling to your ankles and beg you to reconsider, but this sort of display tends not to work if you've really made up your mind. In fact it may make you leave sooner.

The leavee is also extremely likely to ask what they've done wrong. This is so that they can either auto-critique more efficiently, or hate you better. It's clearly up to you what you do here; go for milk, or stick around and tell them. Maybe there really are things that have upset you. Perhaps their porn addiction got you down after a while. Perhaps it was their insistence on maintaining separate food cupboards. Or flying into jealous rages over nothing. It's true that by talking about these things you might be able to help them. By the time their fifth boyfriend leaves because they allow the dog to sleep in the bed they might begin to get the message. But sometimes the reasons you don't love someone any more are too petty to admit to. You can't seriously end a three-year relationship because the person gets food on their lips when they eat. Or can you? While it may be the thing you hate about them more than the dog, more than the porn, is it really okay to tell them about it? It will certainly make them hate themselves and you – and perhaps give them useful building materials for their recovery project. But how can you justify it to yourself? Are you just mad? Incapable of good object relations? Do *you* have undiagnosed Asperger's? Or is their bad habit emblematic of a deeper cause? Perhaps their mother doted on them so much that it never occurred to them to criticize their perfect offspring's table manners. They are generally not well house-trained. They have never stopped being a child. It's *this* that you hate, not the actual smears of ketchup. But shouldn't you be trying to help them? Not sitting there silently hating them for something that's only half their fault.

In a very solemn sense, it's your choice. If you take relationships seriously, you might come to the other person's rescue. You can try carefully and gently to help them. You like it when they do the same for you. You too need to be told that your balding head would look better shaven, or that you should get a job. But as soon as you opt for this path you are embroiling yourself in something quite terrifying: another person's world. And the more you involve yourself in it, the more difficult it will be to extract yourself. You become locked in a dance of mutual affection and disdain. You need each other – no one else tells you the truth like they do and without this exchange of truths the world makes no sense. But it can also be a mutually destructive pain in the arse and this is precisely why you decided to leave in the first place.

Attachment is almost necessarily infantilizing. Being stuck on one person is fundamentally childish. And if you cause someone to attach themselves to you by being nice to them and giving them hopes concerning love, then there will be consequences. You can't just leave and expect it all to go smoothly. They will obviously behave as though they are three years old and you've just dropped them off at the orphanage. You've woken up that baby-like thing in them, and hence they will scream. If the circumstances were reversed you might well do the same.

One serious problem is that as soon as you start to give the real reasons for leaving you are already back in the relationship, trying to take the other person's reality into account and to respond in an honourable manner. You don't want to hurt them and you remember that they are actually a nice person. If they were just your friend you wouldn't even mind the dirty-lip thing. So why should it bother you in a lover? It would be cruel to leave such a sweet, fragile being. You can't do it. You'll stay.

You have to be selfish to leave. You have to stop caring (even if only temporariliy) about what the other person wants. If the alternative is misery, boredom and gut-rot then you just have to take the shame on yourself. There is no flawless solution. Relationships are difficult and loneliness is awful. Leaving is always unpleasant and the gut-rot may get you in the end anyway. Perhaps you *are* making a mistake. You feel like shit too. Go shopping; there's no quick cure for Asperger's.

Try, Try Again

The 1970s was a great decade for splitting up. Everyone's parents were doing it. As Andy Warhol put it: 'In the 60s everybody got interested in everybody. In the 70s everybody started dropping everybody.' There were lots of popular films about love collaps-ing – *Kramer vs. Kramer*, *The Way We Were*, *Annie Hall*. Movies about break-ups have one very serious advantage over ones where people get together: when the credits roll you don't have to think about all the things that are about to go wrong – they've already happened. In *Kramer vs. Kramer* the break-up is executed within the first ten minutes. Joanna chucks the work-obsessed Ted on the day he receives a big promotion. She's sick of being a wife and mother and goes off to California to 'find herself'. Ted is left with their six-year-old son, Billy. He's a crap dad who can't even make breakfast, and he and Billy get on with driving each other round the bend. But as time passes, Ted gets the hang of Billy and they start to really love each other. At which point Joanna reappears and says she wants her son back. A nasty court battle ensues. Both of their lawyers are bastards. They're only doing their jobs, it's just that their jobs involve trying to prove that there's one half of the couple that's good and another half that's bad. Ted's lawyer sets out to prove that Joanna is a dippy slut, while Joanna's tells the court that Ted's neglect drove her away – *and* that he let Billy fall off a climbing frame.

As the second-hand insults fly around, Joanna and Ted can barely look at each other. They both know that it's not really about right and wrong, or who is provably the better person. The truth is that they just couldn't work things out between them. When Ted's lawyer presses Joanna to admit that she was a failure as a wife, Ted shakes his head behind his lawyer's back to let her know that he doesn't see it that way. The lawyers just have to behave as though there's a simple divide between good and evil, and as if their client is on the right side of it. It's a theatrical device, like bursting into song in a musical, or pretending you don't know who's behind you in a panto. Everybody has to act as though it's normal for the duration of the performance. But we all know it's wrong and weird.

Kramer vs. Kramer was praised for giving equal weight to both sides. While Ted's relationship with Billy forms the heart of the story, we can see why Joanna left him. It's a bit harder to see why she also ditched her son, but perhaps you can put that down to a very confusing moment in feminist history, and the fact that the film was made by a man. (It was actually based on a novel by Avery Corman, who himself was married for thirty-seven years, up till his wife's death.) While you are in the throes of a vicious, accusatory split you might like the idea of some experts coming in and untangling the mess, but it can often be very disappointing and alienating in reality. Your legal advisors are just two more twisted individuals who want to warp the story to their own ends. Perhaps the best service they can provide is to make the couple see how ludicrous their sanctimonious wrangling really is. Ted and Joanna spend tens of thousands of dollars on lawyers, and then disregard the court ruling and do things their own way. He gets Billy, and she gets to feel all right about herself. It's a tolerably happy ending – a bit messy and unsatisfying, but what do you expect?

In *The Way We Were* it's the man who ditches the child, but not till the end of the movie. Before that we get to see the mismatched couple shambling through their impossible relationship. Katie is an idealistic Marxist Jew, and Hubell is a pleasure-seeking WASP. He seems to stand for something she can never have, and she is something he's not supposed to want. Every time he tries to get away she hits him with some desperately needy romantic claptrap and he falls for it. But she hates his friends and the way he is prepared to squander his writing talents in Hollywood, and she never quite matches his WASPY image of a desirable woman. It's clear that the whole thing is a nightmare – what's amazing is that they do actually manage a few smoochy walks on the beach before the inevitable rupture. The most difficult thing to watch is Katie's extreme passive aggression. She constantly uses well-worn tricks like cooking and food shopping as a means to push her man around. While Hubell isn't in the least bit likeable, you have to feel sorry for him because of the ways in which he's being manipulated. The break comes as quite a relief – at last the two halves can stop pretending. She can stop ironing her hair and he can pursue his sexual fascination with stuck-up airheads.

You might see the getting together of two individuals as something like an immovable object meeting an unstoppable force. Something has to give on both sides. Love generally involves some kind of transformation. But if the changes demanded are too much, it may not be possible to arrive at a comfortable resting place. In *The Way We Were* it's easy to see that the characters expect far too much of each other in terms of alteration, and that love is the power that is supposed to magically bring it about. They finally admit defeat when Hubell reverts to type and has an affair with Katie's arch WASP enemy. To make things worse, Katie is pregnant at the time. You might say that it was a perfect example of a Schopenhauerian romance: there's no reason for the couple to be together other than to serve the will of the species. As soon as the egg has been fertilized they can both stop trying to warp their beings out of recognition and return to less distorted versions of themselves. When they meet in New York years later, Hubell is working for TV and holding hands with a super-preppy blonde, and Katie is handing out political pamphlets and married to 'the only David X. Cohen in the phone book'. They are back to being the way they were before love made them think they had to turn into something else. This could also be said to be a happy ending.

Woody Allen's *Annie Hall* is a little different in that the characters appear to be far better matched. Admittedly they have the same racial/cultural clash (Alvy is Jewish and Annie is descended from at least one 'classic Jew-hater'), but there's an immediate chemistry between them and no obvious reason why they shouldn't try to make a go of it – other than that they are a pair of extremely angsty neurotics. Woody Allen's films provide us with an amazing array of romantic freaks and failures, a deluge of reasons not to get involved. But what's amazing about his heroes and heroines in that they never give up. His films seem to document an endless series of botched romantic attempts. The people like each other for a bit, before realizing that love itself is just too difficult, that it demands too much of the people involved. When, in *Annie Hall*, Alvy (played by Woody Allen) stops a happy couple in the street and asks them the secret of their relationship, they explain to him that they are both very stupid and superficial. The thesis of all his work seems to be that if you take life – and death – seriously then it will be very hard for you to sustain a romance. As soon as you become aware of your own and the other person's disturbing complexity you won't be able to comfortably coexist.

One thing that makes *Annie Hall* special – and very different from most other love stories – is that the couple really try to look beyond the easy ideals of love and to engage with each other properly. Or at least Alvy does. He can't say 'I love you' because what he feels for Annie is so particular that the words become inadequate. He can't have sex with her unless he feels like she's both physically and psychically present. He encourages her to go into psychoanalysis in order to understand something about who she really is and what she really wants. You could say that Alvy is an exemplary romantic realist – he desperately wants to have a proper, honest relationship with Annie, not just to twit around acting like they're in love. The problem turns out to be that this strategy is every bit as flawed as the hopeless idealism of Katie in *The Way We Were*. If Katie hoped to make it all work with hot dinners and tears and big speeches about 'I love you more and better than anyone ever will', then Alvy pins his hopes on the peeling back of surfaces and the sweeping aside of romantic clichés in search of a greater truth. The problem is that this turns out not to be so easy to do. When he tries to stop Annie smoking dope in bed, saying that he wants to be with her in her natural, unadulterated state, he makes it impossible for her to enjoy herself. When she goes to the shrink (which he pays for) it quickly becomes apparent how much she feels he is trying to control her, the paradox being that sending her to the shrink is in itself another controlling act. Every step Alvy makes in the name of 'truth' – pushing Annie towards literature, philosophy, and endless books about death – is like the negative of Katie's invitations to be coupley and dependent. While Katie offers

Hubell a cosy life with someone who will feed, wash and love him, Alvy offers Annie a fragile alliance in the face of futility and death. If the tragedy of *The Way We Were* is that overblown romantic ideals aren't enough to glue people together, then the even greater tragedy of *Annie Hall* seems to be that the giving up of cheesy, fixed romantic notions certainly doesn't work either. Especially not if one half of the couple is trying to indoctrinate the other half with his particular way of seeing the world.

So why doesn't Alvy just admit defeat and get on with being single? The movie ends with a rather cryptic elaboration of a joke. Alvy tells the one about the man who consults a psychiatrist about his mad brother who thinks he's a chicken.

'"Why don't you turn him in?" asks the doctor.

'"I would, but I need the eggs," says the man.'

'Well, I guess that's pretty much how I feel about relationships,' says Alvy. 'They're totally irrational and crazy and absurd but I guess we keep going through it because most of us need the eggs.' We put up with the difficulty of relationships because of the imaginary benefits. At first glance it might seem like a rather bleak view – love is pretty awful and the thing we expect to get from it doesn't even exist.

But the question is whether the illusion of love is a necessary madness, something we genuinely need. It can be no accident that the joke involves eggs, which are central to the matter of reproduction and sex. We certainly need *real* eggs for something. But maybe the real eggs and the imaginary eggs are not so easy to separate.

Where Would We Be in 1973 Without Eggs?

Actually, *Annie Hall* came out in 1977, but the question asked by the Trachtenberg Family Slideshow Players in their song 'Eggs' still stands. Eggs are important. There's the impossible question of chickens and eggs and origins and how anything ever got there and why it is like it is. For ancient philosophers, the chicken/egg conundrum opened onto the broader question of existence in general. Like love, eggs are extremely hard to contemplate.

It's all very well to say that love as we know it is a fairly recent invention. But we also know that people have been swooning and suffering for at least as long as they've been able to write. And that, before that, they were living in groups and bringing up children, which suggests some form of attachment. While the earliest humans may not have sent valentine cards and given each other chocolates, they were certainly having sex and co-habiting; they must have believed that getting along with each other somehow seemed like a good idea. For lots of animals, the ability to live in packs is an important survival skill. But we are the only ones (as far as we know) who tell stories about our dealings with each other and make a big deal of who we pick to sleep with, and why. So what is it about us that makes us get in such a lather about love?

As we've been saying intermittently all the way along, there is something infantile about love; it's no accident that the word 'baby' appears in so many love songs. The brain chemistry of nursing mothers and new lovers has been shown to be very much the same. It seems there's something about the way humans do babies that informs the way we do almost everything else. One of the unusual features of human reproduction is that we give birth to our offspring very prematurely. While baby giraffes can jump up and wander off, and turtles can even hatch and make their own way in the world without parents, human babies need constant care and attention or they die. Evolutionary biologists believe that the reason for this is that walking upright changed the shape of man's pelvis, making it narrower. Babies had to come out sooner otherwise they wouldn't fit. The effects of human babies being born so floppy and useless are two-fold (or a billion-fold, depending on how you look at it). On the one hand it's very important that their parents like them, and each other, enough to stick around and do the hard work. On the other hand it also means that human babies' brains develop outside the womb rather than inside it. While newborn chimpanzee brains are already half grown, human infant brains are only a quarter of the size they will eventually reach. This means that the human brain largely develops in relation to the external world. Humans interact from the very beginning. Receiving information and reacting to it is something we have to do from a far earlier stage of our development than other animals. No wonder we live in pairs, families, groups, villages, cities, and develop technology in order to communicate with beings from outer space. Our insides are outside. We are extravagantly social; making links with the outside is what we do.

But before we get too pleased with ourselves for being so friendly and nice we have to remember what Darwin taught us about the non-teleological nature of natural selection (that there's no grand plan, merely a series of temporary solutions); just because something helps with survival under one particular set of circumstances, it doesn't follow that it's an indefinitely brilliant idea. A feature that might happen to get a species through a tough patch may cause problems further down the line. Our uprightness is far from fully worked out, which is why so many people suffer hip problems later in life. Not to mention the fact that our success as a species is the very thing that may eventually bring about our extinction. The more we love our babies, and breed, eat, fly, build motorways (to make connections!) and manufacture nappies, the deeper we dig our own graves. But what are we supposed to do about it? Some ecologists argue that we should just get on with burning ourselves out and leave the earth to the trees and the cockroaches. As far as we are aware plants and insects don't experience love, so are far less likely to get together to build the sorts of societies that threaten to destroy the planet. This would be something like the sort of sacrifice we see in Dolly Parton's 'I Will Always Love You', a song about leaving someone you love in order to do them a favour and set them free. (Now see what I mean about evolutionary theory being adaptable to *anything*? Even re-inflecting Dolly Parton lyrics.)

The problem is that we love our world and our species, so are not inclined to give it up without a fight. There is something relentless about human attachment. Some aspect of it seems to be so intrinsic to us that, unless evolution gradually fixes us, there's probably very little we can do about it. In the words of Captain and Tenille, 'Love Will Keep us Together', but it's also clear that Joy Division were onto something when they said 'Love Will Tear Us Apart'. Love is both our salvation and our destruction.

Still, while we can doubt it and question it and write stroppy books about it, love isn't going to stop happening. There is something about sticking together and forming intense bonds that humans as a whole are extremely unlikely ever to give up. In fact, if they did, then they might not be considered humans any more but some new creature. While we might regularly experience love as 'totally irrational and crazy and absurd', it's just something we have to find a way to manage.

Love Isn't Like a Butterfly for Most People, Most of the Time

Without love as a central theme, it's impossible to imagine the existence of most of our greatest works of art, literature or philosophy. Scientists are also quite clear on the importance of love – it's a critical behaviour in terms of species survival. And for psychoanalysts, love is a fundamental human principle – we can only exist in relation to it, whether we allow ourselves to fully experience it or not. While people might criticize the authors of popular romances and the writers of sentimental songs for being facile and slushy, you could also say that they are responsible for creating some of our most important and influential forms of culture. Silly love songs somehow deal with the nuts and bolts of our very existence – albeit in a codified and artificial way.

One of the main objections to romantic songs and stories is that they don't tell it like it is. They very often make love seem like something entirely pleasant. But telling it like it *isn't* might just be the most important thing a silly love song can do. There's something rather brutal about the whole business of getting together. We have the popular image of early humans clubbing each other over the head and dragging each other off to caves, as if this is somehow the bottom line, the minimum courtship necessary. Love of the sort that appears in fairy tales and certain pop songs carries us away from this sort of functionality and dresses human contact up in much frillier clothes, as if to veil the horror of it. But this veiling seems to be what we need in order for society to operate. If we don't organize the world into words, stories and songs we might revert to being beasts. We cling to, club and even eat each other. Silly love songs are an essential technology for constructing bearable links between people – and the more outlandishly removed from 'nature' the better. And silly rituals like sending heart-infested cards on Valentine's Day are perhaps part of this same project. By submitting ourselves to these little romantic rites we are openly agreeing to at least try to treat our loved ones in a civilized manner.

Dolly Parton's songs are famous for being some of the silliest and most sublime of all. In 'Love is Like a Butterfly' she gives a definition of love that couldn't be further removed from prehistoric rapes, or from the domestic drudgery that defines much modern human coexistence. Love, according to Dolly, is rare, gentle, sweet, precious and fluttery. (Don't tell me, Carrie Bradshaw loves Dolly too!) It certainly isn't moany, needy, manipulative, violent or dull. Songs like this can perhaps provide us with compass points for what love could be. They conjure up a picture we can almost believe in. Occasionally love *does* feel a bit like that. Other songs offer other definitions. Some of them are gloomy, some of them are hesitant, some of them are funny. Every love song, like every relationship, offers a different take on the problem of love and, as such, is surely a worthwhile endeavour.

If love is so important and hard to avoid it may actually be very helpful to be guided – even lured – by these often dazzlingly optimistic depictions of what it might be. While we might not actually believe in them, we may need them for something. Love isn't generally like a butterfly (unless you mean one that stamps its foot in New York and causes a hurricane in Honolulu, or poisons you, or deceives you into thinking it's some other creature, or is just very hard to catch), but if it were it would be nice. And this thought might even be enough to keep us going, trying, hoping, imagining that relations with other beings can be rewarding and worthwhile. Realism has no place in romance – romance is precisely a defence against what's real. Love is the fantasy architecture we build to bridge the gulfs between people – and silly love songs are a vital part of the infrastructure. As Jacques Lacan tells us, if you speak about love you are necessarily being stupid. But he also states that the only serious thing you can write is a love letter. Realistically, silliness is all we have.

Acknowledgements

I'd like to thank the people who helped not only with this book, but with my life in general. Very, very special thanks to: Maria Alvarez, Maria Aristodemou, Laura Barber, Martin Creed, Vincent Dachy, Teresita Dennis, Dorothea Grose Forrester, Peter Grose, Roslyn Grose, Mary Horlock, Darian Leader, Antonia Manoochehri, Bridget MacDonald, Laura Morris, Sophie Parkin, Daisy de Villeneuve, Estela Welldon and to my analysands who teach me so much.

Index